One Hundred Messages From Above

For a Rapid Spiritual Ascension

DAVID BARRETO

Copyright© 2024 David Barreto
All rights reserved

One Hundred
Messages
From Above

First edition: 2024, London, Great Britain

Cover and design: David Barreto
ISBN: 978-1-9162111-8-6

www.davidbarreto.net

No part of this book may be reproduced or used in any form or by any means, including electronic or mechanical methods such as photocopying, recording, or as a downloadable file, without the prior written permission of the author.

Index

Preface…………………………viii

Accusation……………………..1
Addiction……………...…………..3
Adoption……………..……….5
Ageing…………………………7
Alcohol…………………9
Altruism…………………..11
Anger…………………..13
Animals…………………15
Animosity……………………...17
Arrogance………………...……19
Art…………………..……21
Atheism………………..23
Charity…………………...25
Compassion………………29
Competition………………….31
Complaining………………...33
Confusion…………………35
Country…………………….37
Cruelty……………………..41
Death…………………….43
Depression………………...47

- Deserving.............................49
- Detachment.........................51
- Devotion.............................53
- Disappointments................55
- Effort..................................57
- Enlightenment....................59
- Ethics.................................61
- Fame..................................65
- Family................................67
- Favours..............................69
- Food...................................71
- Forgiveness........................73
- Free Will............................75
- Gains..................................79
- Gossip................................81
- Guilt...................................83
- Happiness..........................85
- Heaven...............................87
- Hell.....................................89
- Help....................................91
- Illness.................................93
- Induced Abortion................95
- Inertia.................................97
- Judgements........................99
- Justice...............................101
- Karma................................103
- Laughter............................105

- Laziness..........................107
- Loneliness........................109
- Meat..............................111
- Medicine..........................113
- Meditation........................115
- Mediumship........................117
- Mental Illness....................119
- Mission...........................121
- Nature............................125
- Ostentation.......................127
- Past Lives........................129
- Patience..........................133
- Peace.............................135
- Plastic Surgery...................137
- Politics..........................139
- Poverty...........................143
- Prayer............................145
- Promiscuity.......................147
- Psychics..........................149
- Relapse...........................151
- Reconciliation....................153
- Religion..........................155
- Renunciation......................157
- Resilience........................159
- Revenge...........................161
- Reward............................163
- Sacrifice.........................165

Science	167
Selfishness	169
Sex	171
Sleep	173
Sorcery	175
Spirituality	177
Spiritual Treatment	179
Stealing	183
Sublimation	185
Subordinates	187
Suffering	189
Suicide	191
Telepathy	193
Temptation	197
Thoughts	199
Timidity	201
Tragedy	203
Traumas	205
Truth	207
Vanity	209
Wakes	211
War	213
Wealth	215
Words	217
Work	219

Preface

May these pages resound with the call to awaken the truths that have been shared with Earth for countless ages. If God, through His holy missionaries, offers the wheat of knowledge, let us make the bread of inner reform.

Inspired by the sublime teachings of Jesus, as well as the instructions of the Buddha and the guidance of benevolent spirits, the messages shared here invite the esteemed reader to reflect on how we think and act on this journey, so that we may accelerate our spiritual ascent through compassion, righteousness, and knowledge.

Many messages from beyond have already been brought to Earth by the workers of light; however, to sow the word of God is to sow love, and if we can extend that love in the form of fraternal counsel to just one person, we will have had an incarnation that we can consider productive.

May the esteemed reader allow their heart to open as they traverse these pages, choosing their readings not only by the order of the chapters but by the call of each message. Let yourself be guided by what your soul seeks at the moment, for each chapter resonates on its own, offering advice and wisdom in its own time.

These messages are the food, but the nourishment lies in the practice of the good news, seeing the other as a brother, overcoming our weaknesses, and correcting our past mistakes through kindness towards others.

We are spirits; we do not die after physical death; and we communicate with messengers from other realms; yet it would be better not to know these facts if we are to remain inert to the most absolute truth, which is Divine love, of which we are messengers. Therefore, let us deliver these messages from above, for they are the path to spiritual ascension.

Accusation

The world, filled with imperfections, reflects the souls that inhabit it: personalities still immature and flawed, unaware of true love for their fellow beings.

When we witness a small mistake by another, or when we seemingly fall victim to it, we accuse. We call for justice, but in reality, we desire revenge. When we accuse our sibling, our colleague, or the waiter at a restaurant, we do not seek solutions, but retaliation.

We condemn the wrongdoers of the world, but if they were part of our family, most of the time, we would protect them, defend them, and in more serious matters, we would plead for mercy in human courts.

The world that does not yet live under the banner of divine love must eventually live under the banner of divine justice.

Accusing others brings numerous spiritual problems, beginning with the swarm of spirits that will surround us to accuse us at every move, and revenge is added to our karmic account, multiplied by the fault of others. If we must accuse someone of a simple mistake, let us seek justice, not revenge; that is, let the offence be rectified by the offender themselves, not merely punished. Let us remember that the divine laws of cause and effect are infallible.

In serious crimes, let us seek reparation, not the pure revenge typical of Earth, for the stain of evil is not cleansed with a bloodied sword, but with clean cloths. Divine justice, in its precision, will determine how the guilty will pay their debt. Even if the guilty must face earthly justice, we must not take justice into our own hands, usurping the role of God. Let human justice be fulfilled and its laws applied, but above all, let us desire the restoration of peace and seek forgiveness for others.

Addiction

Most addictive behaviours persist when the vital energies generated in the lower regions of the physical and astral bodies are not transformed through dedication and service to others. This vitality, residing in these lower regions, is, in most cases of addicted individuals, a stagnant energy demanding immediate release through the pleasures of the physical world or sensations. Simply put, addiction is the misdirection of this vitality, which, instead of being dedicated to constructive work, is entirely focused on the pursuit of pleasure.

Although many believe that the addicted individuals lack the means to produce sufficient energy related to happiness and satisfaction, in reality, they often generate a great deal of energy, but this energy is quickly converted into worldly sensations, leading them to addiction.

When an individual chooses to turn towards others, helping and serving their fellow beings, dedicating their time to causes that touch the heart—whether for the good of people, animals, or the world—this vitality is naturally drawn to their higher energy vortices, where it is transfigured into love. And love, in this journey, is the compassionate act given without expectations. As this energy ascends, the need to dissipate it in worldly pleasures dissolves like mist in the sunlight.

Although addictions are complex and may involve numerous layers of the soul, the addicted spirit, in its core, knows that only love offered to others can save them.

We should not judge those with addictions, for we all carry within us some unknown addiction. Let us elevate our prayers for their healing and remember that the cruellest of vices is to dress as judges when we are executioners.

Adoption

The adoption of a being, whether human or animal, is not just an act of love but also one of karmic redemption, especially when it involves adopting a child. The formation of families does not happen by chance, but according to specific plans to bring together spirits who have known each other for a long time, helping them to repair wrongs committed against one another and to fulfil missions together.

Many believe that the choice to adopt is a matter of personal preference, selecting children based on appearance and age. However, the truth is that, in every case, the child is already destined to be part of the family even before birth.

Similarly, children born with severe health conditions, such as special needs or significant physical limitations, are karmic redemptions agreed upon by the family members themselves in the spiritual planes. To detach from a child for these reasons only worsens the situation for both parties, as the parents' future redemption experiences will be so significant that perhaps two or more lifetimes will be required to repair the error of abandonment.

Whether through pregnancy or adoption, the spirits already know one another, and there is no mistake regarding the family in which the being will belong.

Even when it comes to animals, the dog or cat with a disability or serious health complications often represents a test for the human being. By welcoming these animals, a person acquires merit and begins to atone for possible past mistakes related to selfishness and inaction. Therefore, abandoning these needy animals only increases the person's debts, who, without realizing it, will have to face more challenging situations to repair accumulated wrongs.

This world is a place of tough learning and healing, and adoption out of love is a commitment that leads us to redemption.

Ageing

Ageing is a temporary condition that affects only the physical body and is often seen as a sign of decline or fragility.

When we resist the flow of ageing, we reveal an attachment that, instead of preserving, often causes discomfort and accelerates the process, sending a melancholic message to the cells that they are no longer as vibrant. Anxiety, not just vanity, is the shadow that weakens self-esteem in the face of passing time, leading individuals to fear that their desires will become unattainable and their acceptance, uncertain.

On Earth, cells age according to the almost exact projection of how long they are meant to last, being replaced by others that, though less vigorous, sustain the cycle of life. However, in the spiritual realm, time does not corrode but renews.

Earthly time is an illusion that, as it passes, ages things and people. But physical matter is designed precisely to do this, to perish in the face of entropy. And the more attached we are, the more we believe that we are ageing, and not just the body we inhabit.

As the spirit evolves, the essence rejuvenates; there is no exhaustion, only the eternal youth of the soul. It is often observed that spirits who have left their physical bodies in old age soon reveal themselves as decades younger, and eventually, in the exuberance of youth, as if they were in the prime of their 20s or 30s.

May we touch the higher realms through meditation and acts of kindness, and rediscover our youthful self, for often, despite a youthful exterior, adolescents may act and do as though they bear the weight of many years.

Alcohol

When someone drinks excessively, they are often not alone, as disembodied spirits frequently accompany them. Drinking alcohol in an addictive manner, repeatedly intoxicating oneself, is clearly a vice, but it is even more harmful to the spirit than to the physical body.

Without a physical body, spirits who suffered from alcoholism while incarnated often continue their addictive behaviours by draining, much like vampires, those who can consume and process alcohol in their physical cells. These spirits do not drink from the glass but drain the aura of the drinker to experience the sensations that alcohol produces in their bodies.

While a glass of wine or a can of beer may not be spiritually harmful, excessive drinking, especially when done frequently, damages the person's etheric composition, resulting in a reduced flow of energy to specific organs.

Despite the traditional or culturally accepted status of alcohol, it reflects the lower needs of the population. Humanity makes little effort to discern between savouring and overindulging, so the amount of alcohol consumed is rarely controlled.

Nevertheless, instead of judging those who succumb to alcoholism, let us offer silent prayers of compassion, for judging others is a greater sin than drinking itself.

Altruism

Altruism naturally blossoms in those who begin to realise that selfishness and bitterness only hinder their progress to higher states, both physically and spiritually.

At times, we may be discouraged by the lack of altruism in others, struggling to understand why they cannot be "as good as us." However, the truth is that nearly everyone on Earth is a spirit at a similar stage, both in terms of altruism and its absence.

To disdain those who have not yet expressed the expected altruism is to fail to understand that they are not seemingly unkind by choice, but because they have not yet learned how to be kind. Recognising that altruism reflects spiritual progress suggests that expecting an immediate bloom of goodness in everyone is a fruitless endeavour.

What can be assured is that no spirit will remain

forever in the lower layers of ignorance and selfishness. All those who experience physical life are in a constant trial that teaches them the art of becoming altruistic.

Above all, may we accelerate our spiritual evolution through acts of kindness, thereby avoiding the need for countless reincarnations where altruism would have to be awakened unconsciously, a process that is always lengthy and painful.

An act of kindness has the power to inspire the next gesture, and so on.

Anger

Anger arises when we fail to recognise that each moment is a lesson designed to test our resilience and patience. Developing resilience is crucial as it helps us overcome anger, while patience allows us to handle situations that might cause frustration. Expressions of anger, heated arguments, and impulsive reactions block our understanding.

A remnant of past lives and a vestige of our most primitive moments, anger, when combated through forced calm—when we try to appear serene despite not being so—signals to the spirit that reason has managed to overcome and tame uncontrolled emotion.

Without confronting anger, transforming pain into valuable learning becomes an illusion, resulting in stagnation of personal and spiritual growth.

Anger reveals emotional and spiritual immaturity,

showcasing unresolved wounds that have not yet been converted into meaningful lessons. This agitation not only obscures our aura but also weakens our energy field, allowing thoughts from suffering entities to influence our own thinking.

Anger can affect our most vulnerable organs in the spiritual body, which may become ill in order to expel accumulated rage.

We should strive to appear calm even in moments of anger. Make the effort to combat explosive anger rather than expecting the world to always be gentle. When we choose to control our anger, events that trigger this emotion tend to diminish, as the laws of correspondence and mentalism work in our favour through discipline.

By reducing the importance of external events, especially those we consider negative, and adopting an attitude of detachment, we can minimise anger triggers. Furthermore, it is crucial to recognise that spiritual progress requires tolerance towards others and the adoption of more rational methods, rather than those based on passion.

Animals

Just as humans are to angels, so animals are to humans. While for some animals are merely sources of income, for others they are equals, deserving of freedom and respect.

The evolution of the spirit unfolds through experiences in each realm, from the divine and its derivatives, through minerals, plants, and animals, until reaching the human realm, which is not the end of the evolutionary journey.

Animals, being one step below humans on the scale, reveal to us that we have just left that realm and that they are about to follow in our footsteps. Younger spirits, animals inhabit the Earth for their own evolution and so that humans, in their highest condition, can guide and influence them towards growth. However, selfishness and industrial-scale control transform those who should be helped into victims of our exploitation.

Compassion, essential for our spiritual ascent and to avoid repeating difficulties in future reincarnations, must be extended to all animals. Compassion that only sees the loved one or friend is not true compassion but favouritism. Let us love our family and place them first, but let the good we do and the protection we offer also extend to animals.

The 'neighbour' is not only the human similar to us, but the spirit that, like us, is a small part of God and that, after a long journey, will return to the divine realm. The laws of cause and effect do not operate only between humans but between all spirits. The good done to an animal generates karmic merit, and the harm caused generates the opposite.

Let us learn to be educators, not exploiters. May we see a piece of God in all sentient creation, and may the animals we now exploit, like ruthless vampires, one day, in the condition of humans, be different from what we are today, showing us that indifference is paid for with mercy.

Animosity

Those who harm us are reflections of our own karma, as we are responsible for what happens to us.

After refining the most primitive instincts in the animal realm, we now face spiritual growth through the way we treat others.

In moments of harshness, selfishness, or deceit towards others, these behaviours will return to our reality, manifested by different people who will treat us as we treated those we have already forgotten.

Divine mercy grants us repeated opportunities to learn to be good, ensuring that we receive only goodness in the near future. However, the blindness caused by the desire for confrontation or revenge against those who harm us prevents us from learning the lesson once and for all. Thus, evil will continue to manifest against us through the actions of others.

Breaking the cycle of evil means forgiving those who have wronged us. This begins with the decision to not seek revenge and to refuse to wish ill upon those who have hurt us, for we know that the rod that strikes us comes from the tree we have planted.

Arrogance

Many people condemn arrogance without realizing that they might actually be displaying arrogant behaviours themselves.

Arrogance is deeply rooted in human personality, as those guided by primitive opinions often seek to impose their supreme knowledge or superior status on others. Titles, degrees, and public recognitions play a role in shaping earthly personalities, which crave a certain level of admiration, even when claiming not to seek it. The arrogant individual becomes accustomed to receiving praise for their accumulated achievements, in spite of their inner voice telling them they are being impostors.

What is true is that the greatest missionaries in this world often appear dressed in the simplest clothes.

Arrogance is a predominant trait in most human beings, with few exceptions. In spiritual and esoteric circles, arrogance can manifest intensely, with many considering themselves masters in relation to those around them. It is essential to remember that the opinions of these circles on politics, society, habits, and culture are personal and do not necessarily reflect the views of elevated spirits or higher realms.

Those who treat others with arrogance and a sense of superiority will inevitably seek a future life of marginality, as the scar they inflict on their own souls requires profound humility to heal.

We give what we have, and the presence or absence of arrogance reveals what we still lack.

Art

Art is the expression of the spirit in matter. The notions of form, beauty, and spectacle are true materializations on Earth of what, in higher realms, reaches perfection.

Art heals through the feelings it evokes, offering us the opportunity to perceive, through our senses, the music that soothes the spirit, the painting that organizes our thoughts, and the harmonious details that inspire us to refine our own inner edges.

However, art is often usurped by the degradation of what should elevate our emotions: the hyper-sensualism that replaces delicacy; the mockery of the sacred that destroys the philosophical foundation of fraternity; and the commercial exploitation of what was born to bring joy to people on a planet still full of trials and atonements...

The incarnate soul is influenced by both benevolent spirits and those still entangled in the thirst for revenge and power, and thus, the art we reflect can be similarly influenced. Many artists are sensitive and, therefore, channel great works, even if they do not realize that their inspirations are direct fruits of other consciousnesses.

Nevertheless, those artists who are poorly understood or marginalized still bring a positive message, whether to help change a conservative or excessively rebellious paradigm, reflecting the middle path expressed by the Buddha.

May the fruits of artists be uplifting, beautiful, harmonious, and, above all, levers that make the planet a happier home. As Jesus said: "By their fruits you will know them."

Atheism

God is not confined to being a man, a woman, or a spirit; He transcends our current capacity for understanding. However, God does not demand anyone's belief in His existence, nor is it imperative to believe in Him for our spiritual progress while on Earth.

Many of us choose to ignore God or anything beyond, driven by an unconscious fear that, if there were a God, we would likely have been observed in our mistakes. Others, in turn, choose to incarnate in an environment that does not recognize deities or assume a physical body with a genetic code that favours disbelief and scepticism. Sometimes, this choice can be extremely productive for the spirit, which in past lives may have used the name of God to control and destroy its peers. In this sense, a life of pure materialism may help evolve without the temptation to repeat abominable errors related to faith or religion.

Through various eras and places, religions have established the dogma that disbelief in God is blasphemy, punishable by damnation to hell or divine wrath. However, at this stage of our journey, belief in God is not crucial. What really matters is altruism—helping others, forgiving, refining negative habits, and transforming into better spirits.

An atheist who helps others and promotes peace is happier in the afterlife than a believer who fills the Earth with verbal violence and arrogant truths.

Charity

One of the main reasons we continue to reincarnate on Earth is to learn to be charitable, letting go of our desire to have and accumulate so that others can be helped.

Charity, often seen as a favour to those in need, frequently reveals that the giver is often the one in need, requiring this action to balance their spiritual debts. Helping someone living on the streets obtain a meal can, in many cases, be a way to repair a past life where you stole all the food someone had gathered. Paying a month's rent for an acquaintance who is out of money is actually a way to make amends for that possible time, in a past life, when you evicted a humble widow and her children from the house they rented. Donating a kidney to your brother may address that time, in a past life, when you stabbed him in the kidney, causing his premature death.

Remorse for the greedy actions of past lives corrodes our mind. However, charity, even when done for less noble reasons, still has the power to heal our mental body. The blemishes left on our spirit create genetic and epigenetic flaws in our astral and physical bodies, which force us, through unconscious remorse, to avoid repeating the same mistakes. The practice of charity initiates a renewal process that heals these flaws.

Charity, whether through money, goods, time, or attention, is the dedication we must offer to our fellow beings, as it is in giving that we receive. We not only gain merits but also settle past debts that, if left unpaid, return as poverty, loss, and abandonment. Those who accumulate wealth without sharing lose the chance to use their resources to create happiness and will regret missing the opportunity to help those within their reach after passing to the other side.

We can help people, animals, and nature, whether modestly or with great sacrifice. The greater the sacrifice made for the relief of others, the more liberated we become from the karmic ties that keep us in worlds of trials and atonements. No cent of our charity goes unnoticed by universal laws, just as every cent taken from others is remembered.

If we have food, let us share it with the hungry; if we have a seat, let us offer it to the tired; if we have strength, let us carry the weak; if we have time, let us do favours for the busy.

We come into this earthly life with many debts, but we have the chance not only to settle them but also to generate credits. Let us be charitable, even with those who may not seem to need it as much. The charity we practice is our greatest alibi, and the blessings of our help never reach others without first benefiting us.

One Hundred Messages From Above

Compassion

Compassion is the sublime understanding that the suffering of others was once your own suffering, and for this reason, you empathize and wish for the other to cease their suffering. The more compassionate an individual is, the more evolved they are, not only due to their own evolution but also because they have already endured the tribulations of existence, reaching a point where they do not wish even their so-called "enemies" to face such difficulties.

In materialistic worlds, where selfishness reigns alongside individualism, compassionate actions that help and save are challenging for those who would assist. Thus, it is easier to remain indifferent to the suffering of others than to face the obstacles required to aid them. However, the ultimate truth is that there is no spiritual evolution without compassion, and therefore, no salvation without it. And this is the salvation of oneself and one's great debts, which, without the help of your compassion for others, will have to be painfully revisited in another incarnation.

Understand the suffering, pain, and limitations of others and help them to suffer less. With each moment of compassion you feel and act upon for a person, animal, or plant, you reduce your karmic debt.

Competition

Competition in the world reveals an immature desire to be better than others, a sad remnant of nature's brutality, evoking a time when wild animals fought for space, prey, and mates. From childhood, brutal competition is encouraged, whether in who has more or who appears better in society, in a struggle adorned by the fleeting beauties of status.

Among the competition to prove who earns more or who is more prominent, there are sports championships, which are the apotheosis of pride. Players and teams boast and celebrate their superiority at the moment of victory, naturally insensitive to others' defeats and feelings, believing they are defending noble causes by protecting their teams and countries. Although sports cannot be equated with competition itself, when there is competition, whether in sports or other aspects of life, the planet's psychosphere is enveloped by dense clouds of pride. Entire populations harbour animosities against each other during and after a match in popular competitions.

The arduous dedication aimed solely at surpassing opponents is a waste of energy that, in more balanced situations, could be channelled into truly uplifting practices. Sports, in themselves, are healthy; however, intense competition is not always so.

Competition is never healthy. As humanity evolves, competitions will decrease, as they will be seen as a disrespectful attempt to overshadow others. In the afterlife, however, exaggerated competitors will feel ashamed of the wasted energy and for having reinforced an instinctive and illusory trait of individual and collective superiority.

May we compete only with our past, striving to overcome our regrettable habits and weaknesses in the face of challenges. And may we sincerely root for everyone else to succeed, as though they were ourselves reflected in a mirror.

Complaining

Vicious complaining is a mental disturbance that affects not only one's mood but also the person's spiritual condition. Complaining is a form of nonconformity with the universal laws, which have placed the individual exactly where they sought to be and have given them the necessary opportunities, both for what was intended for their benefit and for their own improvement.

There is a type of crying that is like rain washing the soul, and another that is like rain flooding and sweeping everything away. Complaining is an addiction, and dulled by the poison of constant whining, the cells of the astral body, as well as those of the physical body, become melancholic and incapable of perceiving happy moments.

Grumbling attracts consciousnesses accustomed to

the nonconformity of their own existence, blaming everyone and everything for their misfortunes. To stop grumbling is not to accept life's misfortunes with pleasure but to recognize that complaints delay invisible help.

Divine mercy is not comforting poetry for dreamers but a true relief from suffering, for the trials we face are always gentler than we deserve. Complaints must transform into prayers, for when our longings rise in hopeful supplication, the universe listens to us.

Confusion

Mental confusion goes beyond mere fleeting episodes, extending over long periods where souls wander aimlessly, unsure of which path to take. In the depths of our thoughts, the spirit retains the memory of the meaning behind planned experiences, while earthly egos stray from this path. Such deviations occur in the pursuit of societal successes, often marked by economic or family achievements. Mental confusion persists only when the ego is entirely focused on itself, emerging in moments of self-awareness when the misguided path is realized.

The feeling of being lost can attract discontented spirits that whisper influences into the lives of those navigating this confusion. However, these spirits merely amplify the existing chaos, without creating additional confusion.

In moments of mental confusion, redirect your thoughts toward actions of brotherhood for others, as this leads the mind back to serenity.

Serve, and there will be no mistakes or doubts in your path.

Country

Countries, from the perspective of the spirit, are formed by those who, collectively, need to face the same trials, atonements, and learnings, as well as collectively build the planet through culture, art, science, technology, morality, religiosity, and philosophy.

Collective karmas are the lessons and experiences that must be shared together, much like in families, but on the scale of an entire people. The wars that a country initiates against another become a karma for the entire nation, being more intense for the leaders of the aggressor country and more subtle for the citizens who could do little to prevent the conflict. The people who benefit from the war, whether through the acquisition of lands or political or geographical advantages, carry a modest collective debt.

These national karmas, when not resolved, cause

collective discomfort for those living in the region, manifesting as wars, cataclysms, corruption, and poverty. Not everyone who suffers in a country directly participated in the cause of the collective karma. Many of those who are part of the nation do not share in the suffering of the majority, while others were guided or chose to incarnate in that environment due to a similar past, carrying karmas similar to that of the people in general.

It is also true that a people can reincarnate collectively in another country, shifting from attackers to the attacked, or vice versa. Thus, collective karma is more related to the group of spirits than to a national flag or geographical region.

Races and ethnicities, although unfortunately considered of great importance by many on Earth, are seen as adaptations of the physical body to geoclimatic issues, unrelated to the evolution of the spirit that wears them during their lives.

God, in His mercy, and through His benefactors, groups spirits so that their spiritual paths are as light and educational as possible. Therefore, countries have their functions with the Earth's populations and are not mere inventions of those who wished to erect borders and walls.

May the citizens of the happiest nations share with the world their inventions, elevated customs, and prosperity. And may those from the unhappiest nations overcome poverty with fraternity and resilience, working for the good of their fellow countrymen, for purely victimized nations do not exist.

Above all, may humility permeate all nations, recognizing that today's servant may have been yesterday's master, and that the poor of now may have been the affluent of yore.

May the unjust of the world tenderly understand that perhaps, in the past, they took advantage of the suffering of an entire people.

One Hundred Messages From Above

Cruelty

Spiritual immaturity is revealed when souls align their most primitive instincts with condemnable ideas, resulting in cruel actions orchestrated by minds that avoid the Light. Although earthly justice seems powerless to resolve or alleviate such evils, universal laws operate incessantly.

Cruel individuals often do not realize that their physical bodies function as numbing refuges for their unhappy souls, allowing them to forget or ignore their atrocities and hide from other malevolent spirits. However, upon leaving the physical body through death, their thoughts and memories will no longer remain behind the scenes, as in earthly life, but will surround them, encompassing and blending with vivid images, sounds, and the feelings they inflicted upon others. They will continuously experience the traumas they caused and may eventually acquire a temporary self-image as a beast or venomous animal, as their spirits will shape themselves according to how they self-identify. In endless anguish, hallucination, and physical discomfort, remorse will begin to be purified, potentially leading to a new life where they will face a form of cruelty—not as punishment, but as a choice to cleanse the past and educate their spirit.

When the spirit finally learns, through its own painful experiences, that cruelty is wrong, it will never again engage in cruel acts.

Death

Death is the final departure of the spirit from the physical body, although throughout life there are thousands of similar, temporary separations during sleep. Often, death is preceded by a long or painful illness, which, contrary to common belief, can be seen as a blessing.

It is common for those who have lived lives dedicated to others to pass away after intense suffering, leading many to question: "How can someone so enlightened depart like this?" or "Why such a terrible illness?" However, the truth is that death from illness is often a final purification, where the spirit, which has been benevolent throughout life, expels its last impurities in the final moments of the physical body. After death, this spirit rejoices not only for the good it has done but also for the opportunity it had to purge the last evils before departing.

Death is a step in evolution, but it is painful for both those left on Earth and those in the spiritual plane when a friend's spirit begins a new incarnation.

After death, loving beings find relief, while the merciless feel discontented, rebel, and continue to experience sensations as if they had physical bodies, through pain and discomfort.

Altruists, who throughout their lives fulfilled their missions of spreading good, find serenity in releasing the spirit from the physical envelope; they reconnect with friends and regain clarity. In contrast, those blinded by material desires, vengeful and ruthless, persist in suffering, even without their fleshly bodies. Confused, they often remain bound to the corpse by past ties and, if they manage to free themselves, are soon drawn to planes of reality that match their unfortunate emotions.

For most humans, who, though not evil, have done little for others or for their own spiritual growth, there is assistance in freeing the bodies, but they may still remain in a state of sleep for weeks or months, according to earthly time. They may also, though not invariably, find themselves in dark regions of the astral planes after passing, where they do not suffer greatly but purge dense emotions and face mental perplexities and discomforts. Eventually, they are led to spiritual colonies, where they will relearn to exist in the astral plane, without the needs of the physical body, and, most often, prepare for a new journey in the flesh.

Death does not sanctify, and the departed do not rest. If one lived a life of kindness, they continue to work for the growth of others; if one lived doing harm, they continue to feel physiological needs, physical pains, and desperate emotions until they decide or agree to continue evolving through a new journey in matter.

The fear of dying is instinctive, but the fear of death is a mental conditioning for those whose faith questions the natural flow of life.

Let us cultivate virtue throughout life, inflicting no harm and building a fairer world for all. Thus, death will not be a fear, for we will instinctively feel that our fate after farewell will be one of serenity and relief.

One Hundred Messages From Above

Depression

Depression is caused by the hatred we harboured toward our fellow beings in past lives. Sadness is not always the result of personal wounds or losses but rather arises from our own hatred, which, in a new life, manifests its effects through depression.

Depression is like that old hatred losing its intensity but remaining poisonous, gripping us to teach that harbouring animosity toward others, even if not expressed through physically violent actions, is still an illness that we must eliminate before deserving happiness in our own worlds.

Forgive while there is still time, and if you're feeling depressed, show love by dedicating your time to those in need. Understand that depression serves as a purification process for your own cleansing and is not a form of punishment.

One Hundred Messages From Above

Deserving

Many people feel unworthy of having or being something, as if they don't deserve enough, and often fall victim to imposter syndrome, making them feel as though they are somehow deceiving everyone about who they are when, in fact, they are not.

Deservingness means having merits, and when an individual doesn't feel deserving, it is often because they truly are not. There are teachings that suggest we should feel deserving, and by doing so, we will attract desired circumstances. However, deservingness is not an emotion or a belief, but a reality that has been cultivated through work.

Similarly, the challenges in life don't happen because the individual deserves them, but because these challenges are the lessons that, more often than not, the individual chose to go through to transform themselves during their journey on Earth.

To feel deserving, an individual must work for the evolution of the world through charity, assistance, and fraternity toward all. It's not about wanting to be deserving or affirming to be what one claims to be; it's about acting to do good, and in doing so, the feeling of unworthiness dissipates.

The feeling of not being deserving is, in most cases, an echo of past lives, where the individual made mistakes in specific circumstances and today, unconsciously, sees themselves as an unworthy being. The lack of merits arises as a subconscious feeling, revealing that there was no effort or progress in that area. The one who stole a considerable amount yesterday may feel undeserving of prosperity today; the one who betrayed and abandoned the family may not feel they deserve a relationship now; the employer who humiliated others may, today, in a new physical body, be unable to become a boss.

Thus, creative visualizations, neuro-linguistic programming, and magical rituals will not turn a person who doesn't feel deserving into one who is.

Let us work and help everyone, so that, even in this life, we can experience the profound sensation of truly deserving what we aspire to.

Detachment

The practice of detachment from material things accelerates our perception of time. As we distance ourselves from materialism, we also free ourselves from the temporal constraints of Earth, where gravity weaves the illusion of a slow march. The further we are from the physical chains of gravity, which also affect the astral plane, the faster our perception of time becomes. Thus, the spirit that is farther from Earth experiences the passage of time much more quickly than those who remain on Earth or in the astral layers close to it.

Many experience time as if it drags on slowly; in contrast, those who feel fulfilled and joyful perceive time as flowing more quickly. Attachment to material things is not limited to tangible possessions but extends to the belief that all answers, solutions, and goals are found in the physical world. Emotions, thoughts, and, above all, our service to others are the only possessions we carry with us when we cross over.

The more selfish an individual is, the more attached they are to material things. So, let us understand that we are, in essence, immaterial beings, momentarily immersed in this physical plane.

Let us cultivate detachment, cherishing our possessions by seeing them as temporary divine gifts, just as our bodies are temporary vehicles in this earthly journey.

Devotion

The spirits who, on Earth, were masters of altruism and knowledgeable in divine sciences often stand out as supreme symbols of religions and esoteric groups. Although recognized by these groups, these spirits are free and, in the spiritual realm, are not confined to the environment in which they were immersed during life.

The great guru of the past may reincarnate as a contemporary agnostic, and the theosophist of yesterday may emerge as today's Buddhist. Or, perhaps, they may not manifest in any specific religion, for they do not belong to groups or creeds, but they will surely return to guide those they encounter, driven by selflessness and love for those still seeking evolution in the flesh.

Spirits who work in mediumistic centres assist the faithful in evangelical churches, and enlightened monks help the needy in Afro temples, just as the legions associated with the Virgin Mary protect the kind-hearted atheist.

The religion of elevated spirits is the practice of the good they can offer to those in need.

Devotion to great masters, saints, angels, or even God is an honourable task that can bring us closer to their ideals and vibratory affinities. However, excessive devotion may lead us to believe that we do not need inner reform, imagining that praising a deity is sufficient to secure a place in their kingdom.

There are many masters, both those who have been on Earth and those who have never incarnated here, but who act with equal importance. Following their examples and teachings, and praying for their guidance, is a sublime practice, as long as our devotion leads us to resemble them and not just honour their memory.

These venerable masters do not require devotion or recognition. Similarly, God, the supreme Creator, does not need pilgrimages or promises.

Devotion need not be abandoned, for in the higher spheres there is a master, whose name is known by many, who resonates with the devotion of millions who inhabit the Earth. However, even he, in his exalted position, suggests that we devote ourselves only to our fellow beings in the field of goodness.

Disappointments

The disappointments we face are reflections of the illusions we cultivate within ourselves, where we unconsciously seek out situations that slowly reveal what obscures reality.

Often, our Higher Self, in the form of intuition, reminds us of the true reasons for our incarnation on Earth. The Higher Self is our divine essence and the centre of all the experiences we have ever had.

Earthly illusions divert us from our personal missions, which often involve forgiving, doing good, and contributing to the moral improvement of the world. When we focus on bodily sensations, acquisitions, earthly glories, and positions, we end up encountering rejection in relationships and frustration in events, so that we may abandon these illusions.

Everyone experiences disappointments, whether rich and beautiful or poor and considered unattractive.

However, disappointment only becomes trauma, followed by other emotional and somatic complications, when aspirations deeply diverge from the real purpose of the incarnation.

The singer who comes to Earth to inspire art with joy and self-esteem but deviates by using stardom to spread vulgarity is still on the right path, as they learn from their mistakes and may one day correct their trajectory. In this case, the disappointments will simply be part of the journey without causing trauma. On the other hand, the actor who came to restore emotional ties with family but chooses to focus solely on their career will face rejections and frustrations that will hinder their recognition and increase their future responsibilities in healing those relationships.

The more we are in touch with the higher spheres through good habits and meditation, the fewer illusions we will have, and consequently, fewer disappointments.

Disappointments are necessary nudges that guide us on the journey of faster growth and will persist until there are no more veils hiding reality from us.

Effort

It has become common to hear phrases like "don't be so hard on yourself." However, behind these words lies an attempt to lighten burdens, as if we are incessantly striving to become better versions of ourselves. The truth, though, is that the vast majority of people are not actually being that hard on themselves.

The difficulties and limitations we face on Earth are often challenges we chose to correct past actions or learn essential lessons. While many of us are indeed severe with ourselves, it is not always with the intention of becoming better beings, but rather to achieve material gains and status. In this context, the phrase may be correctly applied. However, its general meaning suggests a reduction in responsibility and less effort to overcome our shortcomings. This idea weakens the notion that we must fulfil the responsibilities we assumed during our physical life.

Some Western gurus of the 21st century inadvertently promote the idea that sacrifice should be abandoned in favour of an easier life. This mindset fosters a culture of individuals reluctant to confront their own flaws.

Buddha taught that the middle path is the wisest choice, but many interpret this idea as leniency or complacency toward stagnant situations. The effort to change, especially when dealing with our flaws, should always be within the limits we can bear, for we cannot do more than what was already planned before reincarnation.

Effort elevates and guides us to spiritual ascension. And without effort, we do not advance. But let this effort be one that helps us rid ourselves of resentment, selfishness, and judgement, not an effort solely to gain more money or a better position within the community.

Enlightenment

The closer a spirit is to God, the more evolved it is. What brings a spirit closer to God is the kindness it practices. While knowledge is a part of spiritual evolution, it is kindness that grants true power to the spirit. As the spirit gains access to more planes of reality through vibrational compatibility, its thoughts acquire greater creative power, and happiness becomes constant.

Angels possess immense power, while ordinary spirits have little and often depend on vampirisation to obtain something. Despite, in many cases, having vast knowledge, these spirits cannot apply it or access wisdom from the higher planes.

By dedicating oneself to others, a being becomes enlightened. Even if this dedication begins with the goal of achieving one's own enlightenment, rather than a genuine concern for others, it still results in an increase in inner light. Over time, the desire for self-enlightenment diminishes, and true enlightenment emerges as a reflection of the good that is done.

Religions, prayers, knowledge, and psychic development do not enlighten the individual; only the good that is done, forgiveness, and altruism have the true power to illuminate.

The one who practices good becomes enlightened, but must also cultivate humility, for self-glorification and pride are illusions of enlightenment.

Ethics

Those who develop or work with various types of mediumship and psychism must, above all, adopt ethics as their primary guide, for the lack of it drags the worker into the invisible circles of darkness.

Divination, clairvoyance, psychometry, or telepathy should occur only so that the bearer of the information can help their fellow human beings in a kind and responsible manner. For example, when glimpsing an illness or event in another's aura or memory fields, it is more prudent not to mention the misfortune, as the sensitive person may be observing something from a past life, mistaking it for the present, and thus sowing doubt and fear in the other's mind. In other instances, the sensitive may capture the vision of an accident, betrayal, or fight, which is actually just a thought-form, but upon seeing it, they believe it to be a real event.

Oracle readers must always remember that they

bear the consequences of the actions others take based on their advice. In many oracle readings, the information is genuine, but it is often manipulated by obsessive entities that wish to lead the seeker to bad decisions.

In mediumship, the spirit that communicates often has knowledge of many ailments present in the astral and mental aura of the seeker, but the medium should not convey this information as proof of their abilities, as it would only serve their own ego, which seeks validation from others. In such cases, gentle advice and suggestions for good conduct should replace entire and shocking truths.

Using information obtained through extrasensory means for personal gain, whether financial or egotistical, draws the individual closer to deceitful beings who feed their ego and make them believe it is fair to charge high fees for spiritual work and esoteric courses. Mediumship and psychism, or paranormality, are tools for the benefit of the individual and their fellow beings, not a means for material comfort or profit.

Paranormal abilities, such as clairvoyance and clairaudience, are personal developments that will accompany the spirit through all lives from the moment they are developed. Once developed, the individual can never close off these sensitive channels again. These abilities must adhere to the criterion of not revealing information about others' lives, not using information for fraudulent gain, and never showcasing them in situations aimed at boosting the ego.

All mediumistic sensitivities and paranormal abilities demand immense responsibility, and when we stray from the righteous path, we must face the consequences of the laws of cause and effect.

Let us choose secrecy and non-judgement, so that what we hear, see, or feel can be a blessing to the world, without using these perceptions for our own benefit or to expose the lives of others. Let us remember that we inhabit one frequency at a time; thus, other beings are continuously observing and evaluating us. Therefore, let us be ethical, so that ethics may also become our right.

One Hundred Messages From Above

Fame

Fame is a condition that is planned in the spiritual realms before someone is born. Its purpose is to help the individual become influential enough to shape the opinions, habits, ideas, and values of the masses, and therefore, drive the world toward evolution.

Unfortunately, the vast majority of people endowed with the magnetism for fame stray into paths of vanity and narcissism. They believe that fame is a result of their work and that it exists to bring them adoration, fortune, and power.

Some artists may have a vague notion of what they should do, but they distort this, becoming entirely worldly, selfish, and even perverse, feasting on the delicacies of earthly illusions.

Let us strive to be great in the eyes of God, not in the eyes of the world, which is transient and deceptive.

Highly famous individuals are often spirits who

were equally famous in a previous life. Despite their current life being planned with promises of good service before their rebirth in the flesh, most of them fail, which likely leads to another reincarnation in a future life that is somewhat deprived. Eventually, they may reincarnate as famous individuals once again, giving them another chance to finally do it right, influence the world, and encourage progress through an uplifting example.

Fame is not a blessing, but a great responsibility, like an alcoholic tasked with preparing drinks but forbidden to consume them.

May the famous use their fame to reveal what earthly egos try to keep hidden, and may the Light above guide them through the darkest paths of vanity and pride.

Family

Family is the group of spirits with whom we reincarnate to learn and resolve our problems and misunderstandings together. Typically, your current relatives were your family in many other lives, assuming various roles such as parents, siblings, sons, or daughters.

Many of your relatives today may also have been adversaries in the past, reincarnating now so close to each other through divine mercy. This allows both parties to resolve past rivalries and resentments as spirits, transcending the roles of previous lives thanks to the veil of forgetfulness.

The challenges we face within our family, or with a specific member, offer an opportunity to finally free ourselves from past agonies. Rivals or those to whom we have caused significant harm will inevitably return to our lives, and peace will remain elusive until we cultivate patience, understanding, and, above all, love to heal old animosities.

A father who neglects his daughter may have been her abandoned son in a previous life; the jealous mother of today may have been your betrayed wife in the past; and your violent child today may have been the victim of your hands in a previous existence.

Even with a history of discord and hatred, family members reunite to heal the wounds of the soul in the present existence through love. Just as the wrongdoer, after causing us suffering, may one day do us a great good. Even if we discover that the person who did us so much good was the same one who harmed us in the past, the current appreciation has the power to heal the open wound. However, if we knew in advance that the one who could do us good was the same wrongdoer from the past, the hurt would not allow forgiveness, thus preventing the repair of the wrong.

Divine law grants us the opportunity to heal evil with good, shadows with light, and hatred with love. Support, forgive, and love, so that difficult reincarnations together will not be necessary.

Favours

Favours should be done without ever expecting anything in return. Kindness should be expressed even when not requested, seamlessly integrating into everyday life. However, favours should not become a personal sacrifice, allowing those who ask to take advantage of others' goodwill while enjoying an easy life. Favours are opportunities to help others and rebalance our accounts with the universe, but they should not require constant self-sacrifice while the beneficiary benefits effortlessly.

The distinction between favours and charity is subtle, and the effort dedicated to others will always return to us, through both expected and unexpected help. In theory, a favour is an act of charity. The spirit only grows through altruistic behaviour.

Still primitive, we shrink into our egotism and miss the chance to do a favour. The bag we carry for someone, the last bread from the bakery that we give up, letting another go first—these small favours are valuable for our spiritual growth. A favour is the spirit's desire; therefore, the law of cause and effect will bless us in light of the debts we have related to the evils of wills and emotions.

A favour is the individual's chance to do for another what should be done spontaneously.

We should not expect a favour to be returned. If we expect it to be returned, then, in reality, we have not done a favour, but merely lost the chance to settle a debt we had.

No favour goes unnoticed by divine law, not even insincere ones. However, the more sincere, even if small, the more fortunate the individual will be.

Food

Diet rarely interferes in someone's spiritual progress; however, some foods can be nutritious, while others can be harmful to the energetic body, leaving a negative imprint on the individual's spiritual body.

The sun, the sovereign star, serves as the primary physical-etheric source necessary for the healthy life of incarnate beings. A simple way to discern the energetic qualities of a specific food is to investigate how close it is to the sun in its process of creation. The closer it is to the sun, the healthier it is.

At the top of the list are leafy greens and vegetables, followed by fruits, seeds, and lastly, root vegetables. Animal-based foods are somewhat farther from the sun; their formation process is not directly commanded by sunlight but by reactions of other secondary movements. So, meats are energetically less favourable, although eggs and dairy are not entirely harmful. Sugary sodas, processed sweets, medications, mammal and poultry meats, and alcohol are at the end of the list.

Eating is not just about ourselves; it also touches upon those who, sadly, may lose their lives to become our sustenance. Kindness should infuse every choice we make. If meats and the exploitative animal industry stand in contrast to this kindness, those who are devoted to honouring love and respect for life should strive to align their actions with their values.

Although we are what we think, the consumption of meat still has the power to influence the composition of the etheric body and, consequently, the astral body, which we should aim to refine as much as possible while incarnated.

Forgiveness

Forgiveness represents the highest form of spiritual practice in a world where overcoming a wounded ego is one of the most difficult tasks.

Teachings on forgiveness are profound and ancient, and the truth is that without forgiveness, individuals will inevitably find themselves confronting those they haven't forgiven, as many times as necessary until they can finally do so. These encounters often take place within the family, where yesterday's enemies transform into mother and child, siblings, or spouses, developing love through the divine bonds of kinship. The spirit, regardless of its role as a specific family member, will regret having harboured hatred for someone who is now a dear loved one. As these relationships intertwine and love builds, even amidst difficult experiences, old animosities naturally dissolve.

By not forgiving others for minor reasons, we will

also face the same circumstances again, albeit without the presence of those who need to be forgiven. These new experiences will lead us to encounter the same situation, so that we may finally forgive the new aggressor. Therefore, let us forgive while there is time, to avoid further wrongs that we will judge as unjust.

Part of our resistance to forgiving stems from the desire for revenge, which, even unconsciously, seeks to punish the offender by ignoring them, depriving them of our company, and condemning them to eternal exile. Those who do not forgive are attached, bound to the circumstances of primitive consciousness, and seekers of justice, not realizing that it is due to divine justice that they were wronged by others.

So, let us visualize our offenders in our meditations and raise prayers in their images, apologizing for having cultivated hatred against them and wishing them peace. Let us write their names accompanied by phrases of love and joy, and bless their homes and families. Let us use all the means at our disposal to overcome this difficult test of forgiving those who have caused us so much harm.

Forgiveness grants freedom to ourselves, for our souls carry fewer burdens and we face fewer trials, accelerating our spiritual ascension.

Free Will

Free will is the power we have to make our own decisions. However, the ability to decide is conditioned by various factors. One of these factors is the level of animal instinct that an individual still retains. The more attached to instinct, the less free will the being possesses, as instinct does not reason or ponder; it merely follows the molecular intelligence of matter.

Another crucial factor is the degree of sublimity of the individual. The evolutionary level of each spirit determines the extent of their freedom. Although we may believe we are free to make any decision, in reality, our freedom is comparable to that of a child, who can only choose which toy to play with. Even so, the child does not decide what to wear or what to eat for lunch. As they grow, they may choose the clothes they prefer and even vary the meal of the day, but only in full maturity can they completely decide on their style and meals. This is because the power of decision is granted when one knows how to make the right choices. Otherwise, the child would find themselves wearing dirty clothes or eating only sweets.

The average human of the past centuries enjoys limited free will, comparable to that of children, restricted by the egocentric and animalistic nature they still preserve. They cannot choose to be rich or healthy, to move instantly, or to easily create what they desire in life. Their choices are limited by their spiritual immaturity.

The spirit that evolves and no longer needs earthly reincarnations to grow enjoys greater freedom. They have access to different planes of reality, can remember past lives, and closely watch over loved ones; they can decide on their future lives and create the appearance and home they desire. The initiated spirit, or adept, who has already reached a significant level of evolution, can decide not only for themselves but also for groups of spirits they assist and guide; they influence cultural, religious, scientific, and even geological events in a region.

The highest expression of free will is found in God, and in stones and minerals, we see its least expressive form.

Service to others, high ethics, and knowledge expand free will, granting the being more options, ease, and the ability to shape the universe according to their will. For true will and ideals are broadly congruent with the flow of the universe when based on love, which is the fuel of divine expansion.

Let us work to refine our spirit from animalistic instinct, and thus, even in physical life, we will be granted greater authority over our personal universe.

One Hundred Messages From Above

Gains

The opportunities granted by the divine hand are sufficient for each life journey, yet we often find ourselves reaping the rewards and circumstances meant for others.

To those who extend their hands in assistance, we owe gratitude and respect, honouring their gestures with the same tenderness and care. Exploiting those who offer their help, however, is a disruption that will one day have to be resolved through personal sacrifice.

Taking more than what is offered to us is a silent theft. Instead, we should give more than we believe is necessary. The advantages gained through corrupt means will always return, disguised as genuine need. Thus, those who ask for donations without truly needing them are training for a future of legitimate poverty.

Many, wounded by the slightest of offences, resort to litigation. The judicial process, at its core, is a repugnant reprisal, seeking either great advantage or the disproportionate destruction of another. Earthly lawsuits, driven by revenge, will appear on the balance sheet of each person, and all will have to account for their egocentrism and inability to forgive.

In work, the sacred source of sustenance, many waste hours in idleness when the supervisor's eyes are not on them; others shift their responsibilities onto colleagues. Yet, when they leave the job, they demand every last bit of their labour rights, convinced of their righteousness. These individuals will sooner or later have to repay the hours not worked, in this life or the next, until every unoccupied moment is dedicated to serving others.

May we offer our help without calculating each gesture, and may we accept assistance only in moments of true need, allowing others' resources and time to be available to those who genuinely need them. And above all, may we see in every circumstance an opportunity for forgiveness and aid, not for gain at the expense of others.

Taking advantage of situations is not cleverness, but the illusion of those who, one day, will face their accumulated debts and beg, on their knees, for scarce experiences to correct the malice of a selfish past.

Gossip

Gossip, rumours, and intrigue, where others become the centre of our attention, reveal our inner dissatisfaction. By exposing or reinforcing someone else's habits or events, we multiply these energies in their lives and in our own through verbalized magic.

The gossiper feels a fleeting relief, as if reaffirming their own balance, while the victim of gossip becomes the target of ridicule, even if it's presented in a subtle way. Knowing that gossip is harmful to ourselves, it should serve as a personal reminder of our own flaws or of similar situations we've faced.

We have no right to pry into the faults or vices of others. By focusing on others' shortcomings, we become more vulnerable to the influence of unhappy spirits, who may exploit our own weaknesses and push us toward further missteps. Gossip always leaves us feeling guilty, often without us understanding where that feeling comes from.

If we don't spend time helping others, we shouldn't use it to talk about their lives, unless it's to offer words of kindness, praise, or support. We should do with others' stories what we would want them to do with ours, maintaining a respectful silence. Even if we see ourselves as righteous and virtuous, it's likely that, not too long ago, we made similar mistakes, and we are still dealing with their karmic consequences.

Let the sordid matters of other people's lives remain with their rightful owners and their spiritual guides. May we use the energy we would spend gossiping in prayers for others, so they may find more happiness and balance. And may our desire to help become greater than the urge to expose the sacred lives of others.

Guilt

Although it is common to find those who advise letting go of guilt or suggest that we should not feel it, guilt must be understood as an aid, not a problem. Those who feel guilty often do have guilt.

Unconscious guilt serves to prevent the spirit, and thus its incarnated personality, from repeating what it regretted doing. Feeling guilt and embracing it does not mean that we cannot forgive ourselves for what we did in a past life, but rather that we are still prone to making mistakes. However, freeing oneself from guilt will only happen when what was done is corrected. In this sense, forgiveness must be followed by actions that compensate for what was done.

If someone feels guilty for being wealthy, this may be a reminder that their true mission regarding money is not being fulfilled, or perhaps it reveals a greedy exploitation of others in past lives. In this case, abundant charity would resolve their guilt.

Guilt in matters of sex occasionally reveals a past where the individual may have used sex to control or hurt others. In such cases, helping those who have suffered in matters of sex will free them from their guilt.

Even if the trauma seems to have originated in this lifetime, it was likely a trigger for an unresolved event from a previous life that needed to be addressed in this one.

If someone feels guilty when giving orders, it may be because, in past lives, they overstepped boundaries and mercilessly exploited others. To heal this wound, they can seek compensation by valuing those who work for them, offering fair rewards and generous bonuses, and showing gratitude by giving presents to those who do them favours.

In certain situations, a disturbed spirit may intensify, through tormenting influences, another person's feeling of guilt, turning a small guilt into something overwhelming. In these moments, meditation and prayer are essential for a deeper understanding. However, the presence of negative influences reveals a connection to the spirit, suggesting that the guilty individual also bears a share of responsibility.

Guilt is the uncomfortable, yet necessary, reminder that we still carry within us the seeds of error.

Happiness

Happiness is a constant state of bliss that does not fully unfold on Earth, but is occasionally glimpsed in various moments of life.

Seeking happiness on this planet is like a child wishing for their ice cream to never melt. In our incarnate lives, we come to learn to detach from instincts and material illusions; thus, the pursuit of happiness on Earth can be frustrating. Although moments of joy may arise, it is essential to remember that this earthly existence is not meant to provide happiness, but rather to offer lessons that elevate the spirit toward true happiness in higher realms.

The search for happiness through marriage, family, work, professional achievements, wealth, fame, or peace should be avoided to prevent frustration. None of these external factors, nor even the individual themselves, can bring true happiness. Instead, one should seek moments of joy, understanding that they should not be the sole focus of life.

True happiness is experienced by spirits who know neither death nor pain, who have no karmic debts or traces of malice. However, these spirits are not confined to eternal rest; on the contrary, they are the most dedicated workers, tirelessly helping beings like us to achieve what they have attained.

Happiness will come when we are in the higher spheres; however, life on Earth is the time to seek that future of sublimation, not the time to attain and experience it.

Heaven

Various cultures and religions describe heaven or paradise as places where spirits live joyfully alongside angels, God, or gods. Although most religions have a playful view of both the conception of these places and how one gets there, higher planes of existence do, in fact, exist.

The beings of the universe, both in the physical universe and in that invisible universe of which mortals have no notion, live on the planes with which they most identify in terms of the vibrational condition of their densest body. The densest body of an incarnate human is the material body, and therefore, they are in a physical world. But upon passing, what remains is the astral body or perispirit, which then becomes their densest body, and thus, they remain in the astral plane.

The astral plane is a large layer whose composition is also made up of astral matter. The physical universe, for example, is composed of molecules with different condensations, weights, and volumes, such as gas, liquid, solid, plasma, etheric, etc. The same occurs in the astral plane.

The human who, after death, has their astral body still "heavy" will remain in the denser parts of the astral plane, where the surrounding molecules are compatible with that body. If the astral body of the newly departed individual is more subtle, due to an virtuous conduct during life, their astral body will remain in the more sublime zones of that plane, in comforting spiritual colonies that help them move to an even higher plane or prepare for a new reincarnation.

After many journeys of trials and learning, the individual may eventually leave their astral body behind, with the mental body becoming their densest body. This body, being higher than the physical and astral bodies, will reside in a region where form is no longer as important, and where thoughts of love, high philosophy, and infinite goodness reign.

The evolution of the spirit does not stop there, but we can already consider these places, where joy is absolute and highly elevated beings, such as angels, reside, comparable to some notions of 'heaven' that many on Earth believe is the place reached immediately after physical death through divine judgement.

We build our staircase to heaven through the good we do, but we must understand that once we have entered these happier planes, we will most likely choose not to stay, for we will have become so fraternal that we would not want to enjoy infinite joy knowing that we left many others in less happy worlds.

Hell

Hell is woven in the mind, and an individual walks toward it according to what they carry within. However, no being remains in these places eternally, and much less by Divine judgement.

The one who, during life, engaged in barbarities with criminality, selfishness, malice, and violence retains in their astral and mental bodies the dense constructions of what they felt and caused, as well as vivid memories of the wrongs they committed. The weight of these emotions, which cannot be forgotten or ignored in the astral body, leads the newly disincarnated person to the layers of the plane most compatible with their own vibrations.

These places, shaped by the mental emanations of beings with the same malevolent imbalances, resemble the hells described in various religious texts. God, the magnanimous architect of the universe, never created such places, but out of respect for the free will of those who still do evil, He does not intervene in the creation these beings generate themselves.

These places, whose parts can be cold or ablaze, serve to purge the torments of the astral body. The dense emotions, in the lowest layer of the astral plane, are refined and, being too heavy for the astral body, are expelled through pain and suffering.

Some religions speak of eternal suffering, while others believe that any moral slip leads to hell. However, the truth is that hell, as dogmatically and punitively described, does not exist.

Only the malevolent dwell in such places, and only temporarily. Those who have done wrong but were not entirely wicked face dark and painful places, though less terrible than the hells described in religions.

Everyone, inevitably, evolves spiritually, and from these infernal places, they emerge for new experiences in the flesh. As fewer sick minds inhabit these locations in the lower astral zones, they become lighter and, consequently, appear less hellish.

The human mind is the creator of hell and also capable of creating heaven. Let us decide, then, to avoid constructing hells, whether on Earth or in the astral plane, and avoid our temporary journey to these places of spiritual purgation by being kind and charitable.

Help

The greatest opportunity someone can encounter in life is the chance to help others. Assisting our fellow beings is the remedy for the wounds caused by the mistakes we may have made in the past, and refusing or avoiding the help we can offer is a missed opportunity for healing.

The help we provide to others is, essentially, a form of self-help, as we are the main beneficiaries of such actions, which present themselves to us to give us the chance to act contrary to the deeds we may have committed throughout the history of our soul.

Helping our family members is undoubtedly a duty, but true help involves reaching out to those who will never know who helped them, to those who will be unable to express gratitude or recognition. Helping others includes aiding animals and nature, for they will certainly not feel obliged to thank us or shower us with honours and praise for our efforts.

Helping the needy means assisting those who appear to be in the greatest need.

It is not the healthy and happy who need doctors, but the sickest, the most unbalanced, the hungriest.

Despite any fear or aversion that may arise as an obstacle to helping others, consider Jesus, who approached the dirtiest, most rejected, and most leprous individuals, in order to, by his own example, show us the path of true compassion, being the embodiment of pure humility.

May we help those who help others, so that they may have more strength in the uplifting journey they tread.

Help is given in the form of time, food, work and interest.

The alcoholic on the street may have lost a child; the bedridden individual may have been abandoned by their family; and the beggar may have been the victim of a financial scam. Help without judgement.

The assistance we offer today not only heals our past mistakes but also returns to us in kind gestures from those we help, at future moments. Additionally, the spiritual guides and allies of those individuals we help, upon seeing the aid we extend to their charges, intercede on our behalf, even protecting us in the invisible worlds.

Illness

The physical body is the vehicle that houses our spirit, allowing us to reside in the material planes. Every major action we take in relation to it leaves a mark on our future physical bodies. For example, a smoker will imprint toxins and deteriorated cells associated with the addiction onto their spiritual body. Thus, harming the lungs in this life will result in weakened or deteriorated lungs in the next existence, which may manifest early, throughout life, or later on. If an addicted succumbs to a disease related to the addiction, in the spiritual planes, it will likely be seen as though they had committed suicide, for, unconsciously, they worked to destroy their physical vehicle.

On the other hand, those who care for their health through light diets and by abstaining from harmful substances and excessive indulgence may experience a healthy physical body in their next life, if there is still a need for reincarnation in the physical plane.

In cases of genetic diseases, individuals who were complicit in wrongdoings in past lives may return within the same family lineage, expressing similar genes to atone for past mistakes through what are called hereditary diseases. However, as the spirit evolves, refines itself, or corrects the wrongdoing through good deeds, these genes will most likely remain dormant.

A spirit poisoned by negative thoughts finds illness a great helper, which purifies the body and forces the individual to cultivate healthy thoughts.

Furthermore, health is maintained through elevated actions and thoughts. Although a healthy diet and physical exercise contribute, our body will inevitably reflect the transgressions committed against ourselves and others.

Induced Abortion

The creation of a child is something sacred for both the mother and the father. A pregnancy, when deliberately interrupted, leads to the parents' regret, especially the mother's, as she faces the responsibility she assumed in spirit while her body was asleep.

For a mother whose physical condition is satisfactory, the duty to continue the pregnancy is a personal mission sealed in the spiritual planes, not a political issue suggesting the submission of her body or the imposition of a conservative society.

Misogynistic and misandrist judgements are illusions of the physical realm, for those who are women today were very likely men yesterday, and those who are men now may reincarnate as women tomorrow.

The future mother was once a baby, eager to be born, and thanks to blessed circumstances, that baby was able to come into the world through a loving mother too.

Children are, in many cases, those with whom we

had conflicts in past lives; thus, we take on the task of bringing them into our own family, so that the love, of those who will now be the closest in the family, can erase the sorrows of the past.

Irresponsibility in the face of this commitment can be fuelled by the illusions of the world, when parents prioritize excessively materialistic goals, turning the sanctity of spiritual evolution into an obstacle to their earthly ideals.

The unfortunate mother, in all cases, regrets the reckless action, especially in the afterlife, realizing that she wasted an opportunity necessary for her own growth. In the next life in the flesh, this mother may experience infertility or uterine illness, thereby regenerating the spiritual counterparts of these compromised organs; or she may even go through a miscarriage or the premature loss of a desired child, thus learning through anguish that pregnancy is sacred.

The aborted child, above all, is a spirit who may feel rejected or deprived of life by the mother, who in different circumstances may have a debt to them, which could lead to resentment against her. In extreme cases, these spirits may become tormentors, seeking revenge for the pain caused by the one who aborted them.

Neither God nor any entity punishes those who abort, and, as much as these mothers need love and understanding, they themselves will offer, through future reparative pregnancies, the sacred bread of hope.

Inertia

Millennia ago, the spirits reincarnating on this planet merely needed to avoid doing harm. However, with moral progress—albeit still modest—that spirits tend to achieve, it has become imperative for people to practice good, as simply abstaining from evil is no longer sufficient.

Ignoring the call to do good, meaning not dedicating oneself to helping others, is viewed as stagnation. A life immersed in inertia, where one lives solely for fleeting interests, is not just stagnation but a true detriment to oneself and, in a way, to the world around them.

Many spirits in the spiritual planes wait for considerable time for the opportunity to reincarnate. Therefore, the inertia of those who obtain the chance to reincarnate represents a missed opportunity for souls whose reincarnation has been delayed or temporarily unfeasible.

Dedicating oneself to helping the community, nature, and animals is essential to meet the minimum requirement. It is not God or the spiritual guides who impose this, but rather the universal laws of cause and effect.

Inertia in doing good can manifest as a veil of physical pain, born from a lack of interest in helping others, which is purged as a disinterest in one's own existence in the form of this painful condition.

No one reincarnates as if they are on holiday, seeking romance or accumulating wealth. Those who come to Earth do so to evolve through love, which manifests in fraternal actions, even in the simplest prayers for the good of others.

We are not called to endlessly seek out who to help, but when help is requested, offer it generously. If we hear something negative about someone, defend them with kindness. If you crave a dessert and find someone hungry, offer them the food, renouncing your desire.

The greater the sacrifice, the more glorious the return.

It is not enough to merely avoid evil. We must cultivate kindness to truly fulfil the purpose of our brief journey in the physical life.

Judgements

Judging others, believing oneself to be morally superior, is not only a fallacy but also an action that brings about unwanted reactions to us, the moral judges.

Before being born on Earth, an individual chooses, or is guided to include, in their reincarnation plan the situations they will face, as well as the most favourable conditions for their spiritual advancement. It is common for those with few **gross** karmas to choose a life of great suffering to settle their debts with the higher law all at once. In contrast, deeply indebted spirits may go through milder incarnations to evolve in some aspects, leaving many heavy lessons for future existences.

Judging the conditions and behaviours of others, as if we were morally superior, reveals the moral immaturity we still possess. Moreover, it shows that we do not understand that the incarnate spirit is merely an expression of the being, and not the entire being.

Those who judge critically, burdening others with guilt and disgrace, accumulate a portion of the karma of those being judged, as judgement is an obsessive act, where an incarnate spirit connects to another, sending them unhappy vibrations.

Instead of judging, let us pray for others to improve. Instead of accusing them, let us move the resources we can to help them, without interfering in their free will. Let us elevate our thoughts to the higher spheres, so that the brother we consider to be in sin may receive mercy from above.

We should remember that one who errs not only does wrong but also trains to do good. Therefore, let us wish for those who err to correct their ways, sending them vibrations of love as if these vibrations were directed towards ourselves.

May we recognize the beam in our own eyes before noticing the speck in another's, and let us be certain that, if God were to separate the wheat from the chaff, we, arrogant judges, would fall into the chaff.

Justice

While divine justice is perfect and human justice is flawed, it is up to the latter to reflect this imperfection in the justice of God. Divine justice is not a system of judgement, nor does it have courts; it is a natural movement of the universes, which we call universal laws.

Universal laws and God are indivisible; one does not come after the other. The law of cause and effect, for example, seeks justice in the form of redress of action, promoting the growth of the one who acted through the rebalancing of their position in the universe. This is divine justice, as it not only seeks rebalancing but also the well-being of the one who caused the imbalance.

Earthly justice, in large part, is the justice of those who pay the most. The lawyer defending the confessed criminal, the judge condemning the poor family before the multinational corporation, and so many people who seek justice with their own hands, but in truth desire revenge.

Doing what is right is doing good, even if the majority are doing wrong.

Human justice is based on manuals, monetary fees, and political duties. In reality, this justice is distant from true justice and, therefore, will disappear from the planet in the coming centuries.

Let lawyers take on cases they truly believe in, so they do not regret sinking the sacred working family or defending multinationals that greedily destroy the planet.

Let judges, employers, and politicians reconsider their agendas and wish to be truly just and magnanimous, for in the afterlife, the pain from having exercised so much power to judge will turn against them in the courts of wicked spirits.

To ordinary citizens of Earth, reconsider whether the justice you cry out for is the neutral and divine justice or the raw revenge and selfishness for personal interests.

And let us remember that when we ask for divine justice, it will be neutral; it will not take from anyone or give to anyone what does not belong to them. Furthermore, we should refrain from wishing upon others the infallible law of karma when they do wrong, for if wrong befalls us, it is likely we have received the lesson of this same law.

Karma

The universe is governed by laws that seek its eternal balance, regardless of the plane of reality, whether at the beginning, middle, or end of something. Karma, the law of actions, whose reactions occur proportionally to the initial action, adjusts the universes and those who inhabit them.

When we act, a situation of equal weight returns to us. The evil we sow brings a bitter harvest, while the good we plant rewards us with a joyful harvest.

The harm we cause returns to balance the universe and to teach us about our own actions, whether physical, emotional, or mental. Those who inflict physical harm — through theft, beatings, or murder — will experience discomfort, losses, illnesses, violence, accidents, or poverty in the physical realm. Those who cause emotional harm, whether through resentment, wishing for others to suffer, anger, or revenge, will receive, according to the law of return, envy, jealousy, retaliation, disappointments, betrayals, humiliations, and other difficulties in their astral body. Those who cause mental harm, through vengeful schemes, pernicious ideals, and criminal strategies or selfishness, will see the return in their mental body, through disturbances, legal problems, setbacks, lack of peace, and deception.

In the same way, the good that is done — whether physical good, through charity; astral good, through prayers and sincere wishes; or mental good, through planning and envisioning help for others — brings, in return, physical comfort, such as health and good financial conditions; joys and peace of mind; and divine inspiration.

Earth is a great school for souls that still need to atone for errors committed in the physical realm, as well as to learn what can only be learned on this planet. However, the universe is an even greater school that leads us, for all eternity, to improve who we are, through the responsibility of handling the forces of divine action.

Using our free will correctly is rewarding, while the debts caused by inaction or direct harm prolong our journey until we reach a point where there are no more significant wrongs to be atoned for in our existence.

Laughter

Laughter rejuvenates the soul, and preserving the inner child that allows itself to laugh is to keep the light of God alive in the deepest feelings. However, laughter born from mockery or at another's defeat is like thorns that the collector of laughs gathers in their spirit.

The habit of laughing at someone who trips and falls, those who speak incorrectly, or at someone who loses is a remnant of a pre-human instinct that must be overcome by more sublime reactions. For us, it may seem like just a laugh, but for them, it could mean a lifetime of low self-esteem.

Instead of finding joy in someone else's suffering, even when they disguise it as mere embarrassment, let us offer help in the face of ridicule, justice in the face of malicious pleasure, and empathy in the face of division.

The inner child is much more than our childhood personality; it is the eternal child that resides in every spirit and will remain within us after the purification of all animalistic instincts.

Correcting our behaviour is a constant duty, and we cannot seek excuses to laugh at others, claiming lack of control.

May we laugh with others, but never at them.

In the stumble, the misstep, and the humiliation of others, let us find the empathy we still need to cultivate within ourselves by placing ourselves in their shoes. Laughter is always allowed, but when it is at the expense of someone who did not wish to be the object of ridicule, sooner or later, we will find ourselves in a similar situation, so that we may finally change the reasons that make us laugh.

May we allow ourselves to laugh with the innocence of children, without the malice of the vulgar, mocking laughter of adults.

Laziness

Laziness is related to the pursuit of worldly sensations, in a mind that evades effort, seeking only pleasures, even the pleasure of doing nothing.

The spirit carries in its behaviour the signs of laziness, disguised as physical exhaustion and lethargy. Sometimes procrastination is said to be the result of a hyperactive mind, which doesn't focus on duty due to distraction. However, when it comes to tasks that bring delight, laziness seems not to exist.

Rebellion echoes vigorously within the spirit, manifesting through inertia. Fulfilling one's duty is the mark of incarnated spirits, and all must honour their commitments. Although rest is a right for everyone, work is essential to shape the spirit that is still reluctant to face imposed responsibilities.

Complacency often reveals deep selfishness, as the individual prefers to see others acting rather than taking on the obligations they should fulfil.

The energetic body is the echo of the spirit's essence. It is not the chakras nor the aura that induce laziness, but rather the condition of the mind, which influences the spirit and all its denser bodies.

Laziness is cured by effort, even when the will is absent. There is no overcoming laziness without the initial effort to cultivate a new habit. It starts by disciplining the mind to foster deeper thoughts, breaking through apathy, and then acting, transcending the illusory fog of exhaustion.

Laziness is a habit of the spirit, not the body. And a habit is only broken when a new, opposing habit is exalted.

Loneliness

Loneliness is an essential emotional adjustment for the soul, which can last from brief moments to an entire lifetime.

In the forgotten chapters of a lonely person's past lie the memories of countless people who may have been emotionally manipulated, especially in the game of love. A man who once made many women believe in his affection, only to abandon them for another, may now find himself in the shoes of a woman unable to find a partner. Similarly, a woman who used her charms to attract men, only to later exploit or discard them, may now be a man who goes unnoticed by women.

Loneliness offers a deeper healing than getting lost in multiple careless relationships. If the lonely person finds love, and that love happens to be someone they once hurt, the suffering they might face could, in fact, surpass the pain of loneliness itself. However, before that, they traverse the vastness of solitude, encountering all those partners once wounded, in order to finally repair the harm caused.

Loneliness teaches the soul to value the true meaning of genuine connections, offering the opportunity to atone for past transgressions through absence, rather than perpetuating the disregard they once inflicted on those who cared.

All tragic love dramas are rooted in transgressions. However, if the individual accepts their reality and chooses to transform their weaknesses into a means of promoting love in the world, their debts will be significantly reduced, and love may come knocking once again, in an unexpected way.

Meat

The evolving spirit recognizes that the consumption of meat and animal-derived delicacies reflects primitive habits from its past. A carnivorous diet perpetuates instinctive customs, where the animal influence still prevails over the spiritual influence.

The subtle composition of meat breaks down in the body of the consumer, polluting one's energetic body with toxins, visible to the trained sensitive as unhappy cells, witnesses of the ether diseased by the act of slaughter. Meat that nourishes flesh not only denotes a nutritional need but also reveals a lack of compassion for animals, victims of human disregard. Consuming meat does not make a human impure, but ignoring the life of the animal for a meal stains the soul with painful hues.

We should not compare ourselves to our lesser brothers, whose source of energy is still the instinctive hunt.

Humanity stands a step above animals, just as celestial beings stand a step above humans.

Some spiritualists on Earth hesitate to reveal the energetic damage caused by meat, fearing to offend the majority who follow them and wishing to avoid appearing hypocritical. However, they vigorously denounce the harms of alcohol, tobacco, and pornography, as such criticisms target the minority, whose retaliation would be non-existent.

Many saints on Earth still consume meat, but their reasons go beyond nutritional needs or appetite. Humans need not live by all teachings of the past, but by those that remain relevant today.

Those who choose to abstain from meat are not automatically enlightened, but those who become enlightened tend to consume less meat.

Medicine

Spirituality often provides healing for the spirit, while the medicine of the physical world tends to the flesh. However, earthly medicine is still in its infancy; diagnosing the body alone is not enough, just as treatments for ailments with non-physical causes, though manifesting in the body, are insufficient.

Each realm has its specific form of healing: the physical body relies on medicines, nutrients, and surgeries; the energetic body benefits from breathing, good humour, walking on the earth, sea bathing, and meditation in the woods; and the spiritual body is supported by magnetic passes, meditation and prayer, and the intervention of friends from above.

The remedies and treatments prescribed by earthly doctors must be followed diligently, even if the patient is simultaneously undergoing spiritual or energetic treatment. The primary causes of ailments, residing in the invisible bodies, need to be drained through the physical body. Therefore, earthly treatments are an essential part of this purging process. Furthermore, even after spiritual healing, the material body needs time for what has been built up over time to naturally disintegrate.

Medicines are part of the evolution in the flesh, even though the pharmaceutical industry is one of the most profitable in the world, filled with tyrannical patents. Each new drug is a blessing achieved, thanks to the science that the scientists of Earth have been inspired to perceive and develop on this planet.

Earthly doctors play a highly elevated role, bearing the hopes of healing and well-being for entire communities on their shoulders. Blessed are these workers, for honest work in any profession is sacred and, by merit, deserves to be rewarded.

The medicine of the future will treat the dense body, the etheric body, and emotions, both from this life and previous ones, for the holistic healing of the individual, not just the material body.

Medicine exists for those who wish to be healed. And even without the means to afford expensive medical treatments, or when diagnosed with an incurable illness, one can turn to the heavens. For, according to one's faith, there is no call that goes unheard, no disease that cannot be cured, and no mountain that cannot be moved.

Meditation

Meditation is one of the most refined tools that the incarnated spirit possesses to achieve growth and happiness. In daily practice, it guides us, helping us remember the purpose of reincarnation and to walk the path towards the success of yet another life on Earth.

Often, the perception of physical senses makes us forget that we are spirits enveloped in a material vehicle, not merely bodies. Daily meditation brings clarity by reminding us of what we are, not what we appear to be.

Meditation transcends positions and postures, as well as the recitation of mantras or prayers. It is the concentration on the depths of the mind, revealing to the meditator answers that already reside within.

The light that bathes the individual during meditation is visible to clairvoyants, who describe it as a golden cascade, cleansing and illuminating every fibre of the being. During these moments, invisible friends draw near, offering ideas that we take as our own and beams of light that, at times, heal energetic imbalances.

When meditation is focused on a loved one, that entity manifests, magnetized by its own essence or by a spirit attuned to it. The formed image becomes a channel of spiritual fluids, similar to an antenna that captures the balm from the elevated being.

Meditation has the power to heal, and if combined with other treatment methods, the world could be freed from the diseases of body and mind.

Though incarnated on Earth, and Earth being a place of constructive work, deep meditation has a creative power akin to that of entire days of purely physical labour.

Let us meditate, imagining ourselves as lights that surpass the limits of our bodies, for the answer to painful doubts, the antidote to the poison of emotions, and the true perception of reality are within reach for those who can close their eyes without falling asleep.

Mediumship

Most of the time, mediums are not beings superior to others, but souls who, in past journeys, stumbled on the paths of faith or lower magic. Under the light of divine grace, they are now given the chance to redeem their steps, facing the challenges of mediumship and, through faith, elevate their spiritual condition.

Therefore, we should not view mediums as enlightened beings, special or more spiritualized than others. Their opinions are not necessarily those of elevated spirits but reflect the views of common spirits who inhabit the Earth to learn and evolve.

Sometimes, mediums are missionaries, returning to the world to enlighten hearts with their divine mediation. However, many, enchanted by their abilities, may stray onto less noble paths. Some mediums, in the form of prophets, performed grand deeds, while others were lost to the allure of cruelty and power, creating pernicious religions that still perpetuate unfortunate teachings. There are those who, regretting the extrasensory sensitivity they once desired, end up ignoring it, living haunted by spirits throughout their lives.

Mediums must constantly seek knowledge, as the spirits that use their abilities rely on this knowledge to convey their messages accurately. It works as though the spirit uses the medium's vocabulary to express what it wishes; if these words are not in the medium's database, the message may be lost. Only rarely can a medium with less knowledge transmit exactly what the spirit needs, and this occurs only with mediums on a special mission.

When discovering ourselves as mediums, it is essential to maintain humility and avoid accepting material rewards for our mediumistic help. Honours and applause should not inflate our ego, and fame should not be the aim of our work. God, through the communicating spirits, is the only one worthy of praise. However, even the Divine seeks no adulation or recognition.

Let mediums study to discern the correct messages from the erroneous ones and to provide useful foundations for the communicating spirits, and above all, let them be humble and dedicated to redemptive work, so that only the spirituality of Light may use them as a bridge between the two worlds.

Mental Illness

Mental illnesses, in all cases, have their roots in past lives where murder occurred.

Mental confusion and dissociative identity disorder arise from criminal planning and subsequent panic; extreme cases of schizophrenia are often triggered by homicide followed by suicide.

Everything we do to others is imprinted on our own spiritual bodies, making it impossible to harm another without first hurting ourselves.

In the case of autism, the spirit carries deep guilt, often linked to parents who, in previous existences, led these individuals astray into the wrongs they had committed. In this new family setup, the parents have the opportunity to make amends by dedicating themselves to helping the spirit they once misled.

Relief from these conditions can be found in charitable work, where altruistic help to the less fortunate restores the spiritual brains, allowing for a gradual healing of the traumas caused by past actions.

The current condition of these souls is an opportunity to, upon receiving a new physical body, correct their affected nervous system, regenerating the wounds they carry.

The mentally incapacitated should not be seen as guilty, for we have all made mistakes at some point, which we may still have to face. Most of them already bear deep regret for their past actions, and their present life only shows how dedicated these spirits are to the renewing law of love.

Mission

The mission of most spirits upon reincarnating on Earth is simply to learn and spread goodness. However, among those with a global mission, few are called to bring to Earth the dilemmas elaborated in the higher realms.

The vast majority of people, about 99.88% of incarnate souls, carry personal missions designed to promote their own evolution throughout their lives. This includes reconciling with old adversaries, reaching out to those they have harmed in past times, and refining themselves, enhancing their morality. All these tests and atonements are guided by mentors, karma agents, and the spirit itself. Each person's life is their own journey of mission.

However, many might believe they have a grand mission for the world or that they come from a special place with a great task on Earth. Yet, this is rarely the reality.

True missionaries are the great masters who come to Earth bringing light through science, religion, philosophy, art, spirituality, and politics. These beings, often but not always, would no longer need to reincarnate on the planet but do so out of deep love for those who remain here, wishing to leave their spiritual happiness on hold to sow great advances in the world in the form of work.

Everyone is a missionary in their own journey, but missions involving large groups or the world are fulfilled by those we can easily distinguish from those dedicated to individual missions. These missionaries are selfless, kind, intelligent, modest, calm, hard-working, magnetic, sensitive—even if they are not consciously aware of it—and altruistic. It is not fame that makes them missionaries but the roles they play on Earth, planting the seeds of evolution, progress, goodness, knowledge, and change.

Many missionaries still carry significant karma, and several choose to atone for it while dedicating themselves to their mission. Thus, many missionaries may naturally have some health conditions or face other setbacks, just like everyone else.

Being a missionary of good is not about being a saint or having a perfect life, but about dedicating earthly life to the causes of the common good, propelling the world in the name of love.

Divine justice has no favourites, and all the missionaries on Earth achieve great feats thanks to their own efforts to do good, selflessly and without honours.

May we aspire to one day be missionaries as well, thus becoming direct helpers of God on Earth.

One Hundred Messages From Above

Nature

Planet Earth is a school where spirits incarnate to learn unique lessons in a denser plane. The planet's natural resources are intended for everyone's use, facilitating progress during our physical journey. There are no owners of land, houses, or bodies; we are tenants and stewards, with divine law providing everything we need throughout our passage through physical life.

Species, from the plant kingdom to humans, evolve thanks to the habitats they possess, refining their forms so that the non-physical essence of each group can flourish. Nature is home to all species, which evolve and drive the evolution of the natural world.

Everyone on the planet has a soul, some as complex entities like humans, and others as simple energy aggregates, like insects. However, each is vital to the whole, as it is from simple groups that complex ones form, and by surviving and evolving, simple beings, according to their evolutionary roles, can reach the human level.

Attacking a habitat is seen as theft, killing animals is viewed as murder, and polluting natural spaces is seen as a fraud. The judge, in these cases, will be the perpetrator themselves, who will find themselves in the afterlife desolated by the resources they took, destroyed, and deprived others of.

Those who harm the Earth will find the Earth returning to correct them.

Those who corrupt nature with deforestation, pollution, contamination, and greed will inevitably reincarnate under conditions of scarcity or on a planet they will see as a prison rather than a school, experiencing the lack of resources they destroyed with their arrogance and disdain.

Preserving nature and treating animals, both domestic and wild, with kindness is not only an act of compassion but also a way to ensure a prosperous and regret-free future.

Ostentation

Nothing that we possess truly belongs to us: neither the body, the house, the money, the nationality, nor the titles. After our final passage, all these possessions remain on Earth, either to be used by others or to deteriorate and return to nature. What we truly carry with us into the afterlife are the memories of our actions, the help we offered, and the love we shared.

Boasting about illusory goods or acquired titles is seen by the higher realms as an adult watching a child flaunt a more colourful or larger caramel than their friends.

In the act of showing off, the individual becomes intoxicated by the wine of vanity, lost in materiality and ignoring the true purpose of their incarnation. Those who arrogantly display what they do not truly possess, since everything is merely lent by divine law, may regret it in the afterlife to the point of choosing a new existence to experience poverty, thus avoiding the risks of again embarking on the futility of ostentation, having once believed themselves rich but lived in poverty of spirit.

May we use our prosperity to provide food to the hungry, our energy to bring peace to the troubled, and our titles to offer solutions to a world still lagging behind morally and technologically.

Let us be good stewards of what is temporarily lent to us.

May we rejoice in overcoming our flaws, raise our hands to the heavens in gratitude for all we have achieved, and celebrate others who also venture forth. Let us prefer simplicity and the absence of ostentation, for the more we flaunt, the poorer we become.

Past Lives

The continuity of life gives us the certainty that, after the death of the physical body, our consciousness persists. This allows us to understand that we existed before this current journey.

In our past lives, we strived and worked, or at times, failed and succumbed to lower emotions, culminating in the present life, where we seek to do better and face the challenges imposed by past mistakes.

Generally, we do not remember our previous lives because, through divine mercy, we are given the opportunity to reconnect with former adversaries and live with them without the memory preventing us from cultivating new positive and healing emotions. Thus, through new relationships, spirits can transform old disputes into bonds of light, fostered by the friendship and love that are reborn.

Imagine someone you hold a grudge against for

cutting you off in traffic or harming you in a negotiation. Most of us would harbour some resentment towards these people. Now, imagine that years pass and we forget their faces. Then, these same people give you the right of way in traffic or help you with a donation. In the face of this new positive emotion, even if we later remember that they caused us harm, the new emotions would prevent the resentment from prevailing. They and we were the same in the past situation, but thanks to forgetfulness, we could live together again and give them the chance to correct the error unconsciously, healing the entire past.

We forget past lives during our current existence for our own good. Memories of previous lives, filled with torment and mistakes, could traumatise us, revealing that our loved ones today may have been our tormentors of yesteryears. Recalling traumatic moments usually brings back the emotions experienced, making the memory both mental and emotional.

As we evolve, some memories of past lives may emerge, but the emotions linked to them no longer harm us, as remembering a moment means we have already overcome those lessons. Thus, those who recall past lives have likely already transcended those old emotions, or they remember them because they are useful for the present. Some dedicated to spiritualist workers may recall certain lives or past experiences in order to apply these experiences to the good they spread today. Only those devoted to a higher good begin to reminisce, not those with mere curiosity.

Upon disincarnation, we do not yet fully remember past lives, as nature does not make leaps. However, as we evolve, or if we have fulfilled our mission on earth, memories naturally arise, like glimpses of a film.

The life we had in the past, which serves as a foundation for the present life, is still not as important as the value of our current existence, where we can be the best version of ourselves.

Let us understand, then, that we do not need to recall past lives; it is in the current life that we resolve the problems produced in previous existences.

One Hundred Messages From Above

Patience

The time of thoughts and will differs from the physical time, which seeks immediacy and material overlap between all other times. Patience reveals a great advancement of the spirit over matter, as the individual, through balance and trust, tolerates others' time and the multiple situations that arise.

Immediacy, rooted in the depths of our instincts, generates in us impatience, which is nothing more than the desire for instant gratification. Knowing how to wait is not about agreeing with others' slowness or accepting that abstract providence will resolve the situation, but about living according to the real time in which each process must occur.

Earthly matters are often superfluous and not as essential as we imagine. By trying to hasten something or not waiting for its natural course, we hinder the invisible waves that shape what is to come, unknowingly sabotaging ourselves.

The wise are patient not out of habit, but because they understand that everything has its due time and that waiting soothes the agitated mind, hungry for results that feed the ego. Adverse intentions hope that we will be impatient and, thus, give up through discouragement. Cultivating patience strengthens us, not only in a poetic sense but also rebuilds our lower mind, making it less vulnerable to the pernicious influence of disturbing consciousnesses.

Patience should arise when we complete our duty, and it does not mean waiting with crossed arms for events to unfold.

Prayer supports us when patience seems to wane. So let us pray that divine grace inspires us to tolerate, staying encouraged even in waiting. Those who wait deserve what will come, and the more we wait with selfless patience, the better the results will be.

The practice of patience is intentional, for the enhancement of the spirit. Without patience, the spirit remains unable to move worlds through will.

Let us be patient, sowing tolerance, so that our harvest will be of ripe fruits.

Peace

Peace is the deep yearning that we all carry, but as we walk the earthly path, we must understand that we may be searching for something that is not yet fully attainable. The lessons we need to learn on Earth may teach us that this relentless pursuit of peace might actually be a reflection of our attempt to avoid fully living in the real world.

Peace differs from tranquillity. Peace blossoms when our actions and well-being remain steadfast, even in the face of tension, allowing nothing to divert us from our true purposes. Tranquillity, on the other hand, may be the simple absence of interaction with the outside world, where the individual often isolates or retreats to places of little activity to avoid confrontation and the chaos of life.

We come to this world to evolve in areas where we are still primitive: in our tendency to criticize, blame others, complain about everything in the city, and deal with difficult co-workers. Choosing a more tranquil life may benefit the body, but it will not always benefit the spirit. A break, holidays, or early retirement is not harmful to the soul, but service to others must continue even after the sacred time of physical restoration.

Peace is something we will achieve when we free ourselves from the cycles of reincarnation on Earth; and even then, we will continue to work to help our loved ones who still face the inevitable realities of physical life.

Inner peace exists regardless of external factors. It must be cultivated, not sought. Therefore, let us seek peace, but understand that aspiring to a completely tranquil life may not fill the gaps we came here to heal.

Plastic Surgery

Cosmetic surgery is not merely an act of vanity; it can serve as a true balm, offering relief and healing when done with consideration.

Excessive vanity, which seeks radical changes or the exaltation of sensual attributes, often reflects a discontent with life's purposes, lost under the influence of the world of forms and illusions. However, cosmetic surgeries aimed at correcting features or enhancing appearance, even if seemingly superficial, can act as a positive psychological boost, capable of catalysing the necessary behavioural transformation.

Physical appearance, while not as important as it is often perceived, is relevant in the current evolutionary stage of human beings on Earth. Self-esteem, damaged through many past lives and in one's current childhood, can be restored through an aesthetic procedure when willpower or mental commands alone are not yet sufficient to effect change. Aesthetic surgery then becomes a ritual that initiates an individual into a new journey, far from being reproachable or superficial.

When the pursuit of beauty becomes excessive, believing that the body is the greatest asset and appearance the only measure of worth, aesthetic procedures can become an enemy, suppressing internal growth by overemphasising the external.

Aesthetic beauty is part of the divine balance in the worlds of forms, and both in the physical Earth and in the astral planes, appearance plays a vital role in building divine expressions.

The harm lies in using beauty to do wrong or as a symbol of arrogance toward those less fortunate. The wealthy are not evil unless they use their power to dominate. The famous are not sinners unless they use their fame to maliciously influence others. The beautiful are not cynical unless they use their looks to manipulate or humiliate others.

In the pursuit of spiritual growth, we encounter many phases involving money, beliefs, and appearances. We have the chance to evolve at every moment, balancing these aspects.

Cosmetic surgery does not harm the spiritual body, but arrogance and judgment have the power to make us so ugly that no procedure on Earth could remedy it.

Politics

On Earth, where primitive emotions and greed still prevail, politics is like a double-edged sword—capable of carving out progress, but equally able to wound the vulnerable with its sharp swings.

The resources and powers granted to someone, in spiritual realms, are a monumental test, as the responsibility of making decisions for so many people is immense. Caring for the collective good and making decisions for the masses should be an act of personal dedication, free from traits of ultra-conservative totalitarianism or authoritarian communism.

Earthly hierarchies often rise on fragile foundations, where the least prepared occupy high positions, while the noble-hearted are frequently relegated to the margins, far from the power that should serve the people.

Those who use power to control based on their fears and prejudices, treating the people as mere pieces or numbers, will eventually have to account for every life harmed.

The corrupt politician, who diverts resources from a region, whether in groups or individually, will reincarnate in the same place to face poverty and scarcity, and after that life, will likely return with the mission to compensate for what was taken from others, dedicating themselves entirely to helping the needy.

Divine justice permeates all systems of the worlds, and what is taken from the people who serve will be taken from you, while what is given through constructive work for the needy will be your credit for eternity.

All political systems are destined to fail on a planet still marked by selfishness. It is not the right, the left, the centrists, or the extremists who will transform the world, but the fraternal feeling in everyone, where we see each other as blood brothers and sisters.

When we criticize the corrupt politician, we should consider whether we are proportionally corrupt as well. And when we wish ill upon those in power, let us remember the moments when we were responsible for something that negatively affected others.

Bless the politicians, for the spiritual responsibility they carry is immense, and much will be demanded of them in the afterlife.

May the examples in politics be those who led with love and fraternity, like Buddha and Jesus did, who, although not politicians, influenced the masses and, instead of dominating or forcing acceptance of their ideas, treated people as equals, inspiring detachment and compassion.

One Hundred Messages From Above

Poverty

Poverty is a sublime school for the spirit, offering it the path to face earthly difficulties that untie the bonds of material attachment. The lack of financial resources is not always a punishment or a reflection of a selfish past, but also a choice of the spirit itself, which understands that, in poverty, it will find more chances to return to the spiritual homeland without the debts of a life of opulence, where the risk of not helping those in need would be great.

The poor are more likely to relate to people for who they truly are, while the rich often question whether their friendships and relationships are based on their possessions and status. The poor have little, and on their deathbed, care little about the goods they leave behind, while the rich may resist more as they see their great wealth going to others in a world to which they will no longer have access.

Life on Earth is brief, and possessions are fleeting. Poverty, from a spiritual perspective, is seen as a course without distractions, not as a painful trial. Many who are poor today were once rich in past lives, and after failing in all of them due to selfishness, they chose poverty as a redemptive friend.

It is not necessary to give up the resources or the great sums we eventually earn or inherit, but it is essential to understand that poverty is a blessing in disguise, while wealth carries with it a great responsibility. We should not aim to be poor, but we must recognize that poverty is often a purifying condition, which, though it tires the body, relieves the mind and, above all, purifies the spirit.

Prayer

Prayer carries a profound power, often overlooked by those who fail to perceive its means of action. In moments of anguish, suffering, and sadness, a sincere prayer, free from memorization and formalities, not only elevates the spirit but also attracts benevolent entities that help us.

Every prayer is heard and considered, whether spoken by innocent children or by those regarded as nefarious criminals. The difference lies in the responses: some are delayed for the person's own good, others are immediately embraced, and still others are discarded for being selfish or extremely frivolous.

Prayers are gathered and discussed among friendly spirits and the high-ranking guardians responsible for our spiritual group. Each response is offered based on merit, karma, and what would be most beneficial for our spiritual progress.

Even when we pray for the healing of someone who passes away, we should not believe that our plea was ignored. The soul that has departed may be receiving, at that very moment, the healing and relief we asked for in our moments of prayer.

Prayer does not belong to the religions of the world, but to all souls who plead for help, being heard by divine mercy through fraternal helpers. Mantras and memorized prayers also bring forth divine balms, as long as they are done with tenderness and faith.

A simple prayer has the power to dissolve, in the spiritual realms, the darkest of magics.

One day, all those who are now on Earth as simple incarnated humans will grow and assist those who call for help from the heavens. Thus, may our life on Earth allow us to practice compassion and selfless aid to others, for every angel was once a simple person who, by ceaselessly helping those in need, became an angel.

Sincere prayer and loving invocation are the voice of the spirit, singing while incarnated in the physical body.

Pray for yourself and for others, for all your prayers will return to you through the intercession of higher beings in your most dramatic causes.

Promiscuity

Promiscuity, akin to smoking and alcoholism, may be recognised as a form of addiction. The pursuit of immediate physical pleasures often distorts one's perception of reality, leading life to be seen as a collection of fleeting delights focused on momentary gratification.

In this addiction, the astral body of the addicted person is composed of a dense matter, which keeps them bound to the lower astral plane, both during physical sleep and after death.

Promiscuity does not reveal an evil or selfish person, but still, someone who demonstrates deep inconsistency by not recognizing in others the sibling they are, denying them the care and attention they deserve – things that promiscuity itself prevents.

The promiscuous person, besides becoming addicted, drags others into their web, perpetuating promiscuity and contributing to others' addictions, like someone sharing a bottle of alcohol or a pack of cigarettes, instead of helping their fellow to break free from the addiction.

The habits that fuel promiscuity, such as degrading films and scandalous conversations about others' bodies, are also corrosive to those who make these things part of their lives, poisoning their mental bodies and densifying their astral bodies.

The astral body itself tends to remain in promiscuity, as it desires to continue being dense. It is the task of the higher mind to overcome these heavier desires. Overcoming promiscuity is a gradual process, different from chemical addictions.

Seeing others as spirits, and not just as bodies, is the higher path.

Life's pleasures are not condemnable, but the excesses that addict and degrade both the seeker and the one found are heavy chains that bind us to the millennia-old sensualist instinct.

Psychics

Exercises to develop psychic gifts or paranormal faculties are a journey of blessings when approached with wisdom, but a dangerous game of folly when undertaken out of mere mischief.

The awakening of abilities such as clairvoyance and clairaudience can occur through one's practices, regardless of intentions or the spirit's level of evolution. Thus, even narcissists and manipulators can develop these skills without moral growth. However, the worse the misuse of these abilities, the more deeply one will feel the burden of the extraphysical world.

Some imagine that by acquiring clairvoyance and clairaudience, they will only be greeted by luminous spirits, see pleasurable futures, and hear the voices of their spiritual guides and other higher entities. Yet, the reality is different: they will also hear screams, insults, and disturbing noises that haunt them during sleep. They will have visions of shadows, non-physical insects, and anguished spirits. On the streets, they will witness beings with grotesque appearances; in butcheries, they will see zombies; and in bars, a terrifying mafia.

Even the most generous hearts and well-intentioned souls must be aware that, living in a world still filled with afflictions, they will see, hear, and feel more frequently the vibrations of those who suffer, thereby assuming the responsibility to help when possible, but also the need to protect themselves.

Everyone can enhance their paranormal and sensory perceptions, but many end up bitterly regretting their pursuit, as once cultivated, such abilities persist until the moment of physical liberation.

The higher our intentions in psychic development, the more we will be surrounded by protection and enlightened friends.

May our psychic journey be guided by ethics, so that we do not expose others or divert their choices; by non-judgment, so that we do not consider ourselves wiser than others; and by the true desire to be an incarnate spirit, rather than just an incarnate being who believes they have a spirit.

Relapse

Often seen as a weakness, relapse is actually part of the process of inner transformation.

One who relapses into various addictions is, in truth, a warrior still engaged in their final battles.

Many of the addictions we have today may have been acquired centuries ago, and even those acquired in the current life are deeply ingrained in many layers of our being. Addictions and their temptations alter our immaterial mind, as well as the spirit and the nervous and hormonal systems of the physical body. Thus, the battle against addiction takes place across all these fields, one at a time.

An individual who, through great inner strength, overcomes addiction but experiences a relapse is still a victor. They are on the path to victory. It may be that they have eradicated the addiction from the physical body and even the astral body, but remnants may still linger in the lower mental body. Alternatively, they might have removed all traces of the addiction from this life, but if they had the same addiction in past lives, that information and the associated emotions may resurface in this life to be healed in the present.

Relapse is not a return to the starting point. It is simply one of the final stages of the inner transformation process aimed at elevating the spirit. Let us not be discouraged by relapse, for God provides us with endless opportunities to improve, without judgment.

Relapse does not signify weakness, as weakness is found in those who give up on themselves in the face of life's trials. The temptations that lead us back to addiction are not stronger than we are; they merely reveal parts of the soul where that addiction or unhappy habit still exists.

Let us love ourselves after a relapse, knowing that it is always a final step in our process of self-healing.

Reconciliation

Driven by pride, we distance ourselves from those with whom we've had disagreements, considering them enemies. Even when we say we forgive them, we prefer to keep our distance, believing it will bring us more peace. However, reconciliation is the only true remedy for what has occurred. Situations of conflict or deep disappointment with someone arise so that we can finally release that karma, choosing reconciliation when an unfortunate misunderstanding happens.

We mask our perpetual separation with justifications about preserving our integrity or self-respect, leaving the situation to chance and time, under the illusion that both will dissolve the relationship and the wounds of the past. The trends of the world deceive us, exaggerating our individuality and fuelling excessive personal boundaries, encouraging us to avoid difficulties and reject people in the name of a fictitious self-love. By following these malicious agendas, we become shallow, evading any effort to truly reform our spirit.

The friend who hurt us deserves forgiveness, and the one who was hurt must seek reconciliation. The responsibility falls on both, not just on the one who caused the conflict. Let us remember that karma is the situation we live through, whose original cause may have come from ourselves, in a time perhaps long forgotten.

Children wronged by their parents have the duty to forgive and reconcile with them, for the intolerant father or indifferent mother are often the siblings we once abandoned or the child who endured our punishments in a distant past.

A spouse who betrays but sincerely repents deserves a second chance, for all are prone to relapses and stumbles. It is through guilt for our mistakes that we grow.

Forgive, without being guided by the deceptions of pride or the expectations of a society that, like cunning foxes, eagerly awaits the end of a romance, ready to feast on the misery of another's tragedy.

Reconciliation is a noble act of love and understanding of divine laws. We do not need to subject ourselves to humiliating or uncomfortable situations to maintain so-called toxic relationships, but it is our duty to remedy the past with the gift of reconciliation.

Never go to bed with unresolved quarrels; resolve them kindly before you sleep.

Let us reconcile today, so we do not have to return to the flesh tomorrow in search of a redeeming reunion.

Religion

Religion is a celestial instrument, sent by the highest friends of Earth, so that we may absorb teachings compatible with the trials and atonements we need to face. It arises in places where a large population, in need of these teachings, has collectively reincarnated, like an antidote near the poison.

Religion forms a sacred trinity alongside science and philosophy. To avoid a life that is excessively materialistic or contrary to divine laws, the spirit, when possible, chooses to be born with a predisposition towards religiosity, in an environment where religion is an essential part of the culture. In this way, the spirit will attempt self-correction through religion, its doctrines, dogmas, and even sectarianism. However, those who have misused religion in a wrongful or fanatical manner often opt, or are advised, to be born into atheist or materialistic households, or with a genetic predisposition towards scepticism, to avoid falling into the same error again. Other atheists, and thus irreligious individuals, are simply the result of their own choice prior to reincarnation, stemming from the lack of necessity to engage with religion and its occasional archaic or dogmatic flavours.

Religion is a great school, where many primitive spirits pass through before receiving other teachings. On Earth, it has the task of distancing individuals from their animal instincts, offering them beliefs that prompt reflection on something beyond worldly instincts and matter, helping them to develop their higher mental capacities before being immersed in deeper philosophical, science and spiritual teachings.

Although many religions have been distorted by selfish leaders and vain tyrants, the same often occurs with the world's philosophies and sciences, which aim to control the planet through military and financial power. Nevertheless, science guides our senses, philosophy shapes our reasoning, and religion directs our emotions.

Being religious is not essential for spiritual evolution; however, the religion of each people reflects, in all aspects, how primitive or advanced that society is.

But above all, one who cultivates compassion has no need for religion.

Renunciation

Whenever an individual on Earth discovers the true purpose of their incarnation, renunciation presents itself, hand in hand with that revelation. At first, renunciation may seem like the collapse of everything the person has sought and believed in. It then emerges as an identity crisis and a dissatisfaction with life, as things start to lose their meaning.

The pursuit of money, possessions, and status, fleeting pleasures, self-destructive habits, and decisions regarding others... gradually, the individual realises they must renounce or reduce all of this, for these values no longer hold significance. The spirit yearns for something greater.

It is challenging to let go of what we have always believed in and sought, as we are still attached to the familiar. However, we cannot serve two masters.

The decision to renounce may begin in one existence but is often completed in future incarnations. Let us renounce angry behaviours, which deceive us with the false promise of gaining others' respect. Let us forsake greed, which tricks us into thinking we must only care for ourselves, reserving concern for others only when convenient. And let us free ourselves from addictions, which flood us with the lie that no other habits are as pleasurable.

To be who we truly are means expressing the essence of the spirit, not the desires of the flesh. Renunciation activates the centres of true spiritual expression, manifesting in the glow of an energy vortex in the throat area.

All masters, at one time, renounced human passions and dramas to dedicate themselves to the edification of universal love.

May renunciation in our lives happen sooner rather than later, even if it is little by little. And may we understand that when life seems meaningless, or when past pursuits no longer bring happiness, it is the truth of the spirit calling us to renunciation.

Resilience

Facing life's obstacles is a daunting task, as it demands strength and balance from us when circumstances slip beyond our control. However, resilience reflects that the foundations upon which we build our lives are solid and firm.

To be resilient is to understand that challenges will arise repeatedly, but with inner strength, we will be able to overcome them, thus building strong foundations. These foundations, however, require us to remain steadfast during adversity. If we lack patience and faith to face the minor setbacks, we are not yet ready to take higher steps on the spiritual path.

The resilient one purifies the impurities of the astral body, knowing that rebellion and lack of control in the face of opposition are marks of instinctive immaturity, like a child wanting dessert before lunch.

Our astral bodies tend toward impatience and revolt, but once we overcome these reactions, we become resilient, as our higher mental identity becomes our behavioural compass.

Resilience, like patience, is built gradually, each time we choose to take a deep breath and try again, or when we realise that setbacks are necessary for the maturation of our projects and goals, refining the final result.

We must nurture our resilience daily, viewing everyday obstacles as opportunities for growth. The spirit's maturation only unfolds when we embrace true resilience, for no one can expect great achievements or fulfilled dreams if they falter at minor setbacks. These smaller challenges serve as preparation for greater things, if we see them as lessons rather than as suffering.

That our resilience in our spiritual journey are founded on a rock, for tomorrow we will thank our today's principles.

Above all, let us practice resilience with people, for they are often the key players in the theatre of our struggles; as the Buddha wisely taught, "Conquer anger with love, evil with good, the miser with generosity, and the liar with truth."

Life in the flesh is not easy, but it will certainly be worth it when we overcome adversities, as each victory brings us closer to true spiritual maturity.

Revenge

Frustration from an offence or the feeling of humiliation from something done against us can awaken the desire for revenge, as if this could heal the wrong done to us. However, revenge marks the loss of a precious opportunity for growth, a moment when we could have ascended a step in the journey of sublimation, leaving behind the baseness of wild behaviour.

Taking revenge gives voice to the remaining savagery in our spirits, so attuned to the plane of existence we inhabit. By seeking revenge, we strengthen the ties to our instinctual past, failing to choose the tolerance that elevates the spirit. The more we indulge in revenge or respond to offences and insults, the more these events repeat, as they become lessons that will eventually need to be overcome.

By forgiving or striving not to retaliate, regardless of the reason, we pass the test.

And by overcoming this test, we free ourselves from the need to face that specific lesson again, conquering the animalistic inclination for revenge. We must understand that the one who attacks is soul-sick, and according to the divine laws of cause and effect, will have to face situations similar to those they caused, without us needing to enforce that justice.

May we realize that it is not others who insult us, but something within us that reacts to others' words and actions, making us feel offended.

Stopping communication with someone who has offended us or caused harm is revenge; failing to perform a kindness for someone who has been aggressive or offensive is revenge; speaking ill of those who have tarnished our image is revenge. Let us choose forgiveness, which, however difficult, is the only path to free ourselves from the chains of human primitivism.

Let us decide to rise, rather than remain at the low levels of those who attack. Let us choose not to attack or retaliate, but to give less importance to the unpleasant situation, inspired by the beloved Jesus, who was on Earth solely to show us the example of loving our neighbour as ourselves, instantly forgiving those who offended, accused, and crucified Him.

Reward

When we perform a good deed for someone, we often expect some form of reciprocation. Directly or indirectly, we imagine that the person benefited will reward us with a future favour or gesture of appreciation. However, we may not realize that the good we have done could, in fact, be the settling of a debt of our own.

This debt does not need to be directly related to the person who benefited from our action but rather to a deeper and more personal matter. In many cases, the kindness we offer serves to alleviate the harm we may have caused previously; therefore, a reward, if needed, would imply that others are indebted to us, which rarely happens.

When someone benefits us, gifts us, or sacrifices for us, we feel the need to reciprocate this gesture. This is a noble feeling of gratitude and affection. However, if the person who helped us does not accept the reward, either out of politeness or because they feel no compensation is necessary, we should express our gratitude in other ways. We can honour this gesture by helping others, such as strangers or animals, allowing the energy of kindness to continue flowing. Still, the true reward is the materialization of recognition.

What is ours will come to us, whether given or not by those we have helped. However, let us avoid pettiness, which calculates favours as if they were commercial transactions.

When we think of rewarding someone for a specific help, we are actually settling a much older debt.

Similarly, when expecting someone to reward us for a favour or help, we mistakenly believe we are in credit while the other is in debt.

May our conscience guide us to reward those who help us while expecting nothing in return from those to whom we offer our assistance. We do this not to avoid disappointment but to always be the last link in the chain of kindness, allowing the flow of generosity to continue freely and without restraint.

Sacrifice

Earth is like a school where we strive for success through countless trials, each designed to teach us something new or correct past mistakes. However, many seek easy paths, avoiding the sacrifices necessary for genuine spiritual advancement.

In the school of life, we are called to dedicate time and energy to our studies and duties to overcome the challenges presented to us. Passing these tests requires sacrifice, however minor for each lesson, but many have become accustomed to believing that everything should be easy. If something isn't simple, it should not come at the cost of personal sacrifice. This mindset has left humanity stagnant, unable to progress spiritually.

The doctors of comfort in the world often say things like "don't be too hard on yourself" or "give yourself a break." However, the truth is that humanity has become complacent with this leniency for centuries. We do not need to sacrifice ourselves to the point of illness, starvation, or suicide, but it is imperative to make genuine efforts and sacrifices to face the challenges we chose before reincarnating. Even so, these challenges are tempered, as our spiritual guides, before our reincarnation, understood that we would not be able to overcome everything we wished to face in life when planning our journey.

We have lived many physical lives, often repeating the same tests we have failed to overcome. Small sacrifices, however, have the power to free us from the cycle of facing the same challenges repeatedly.

Sacrifice means choosing what is right, even when it is painful; even if isn't done by the majority.

By dedicating our energy and time to helping this world and its inhabitants, we will finally graduate and advance to a higher school.

Those who avoid sacrifice remain stuck in the mundane, while those who truly dedicate themselves will find the spiritual progress they seek.

Science

Alongside philosophy and religion, science stands as one of the great pillars of humanity, each driving nations in its own time, according to the needs of each people. More than a human discovery, science reveals itself in all planes of reality, with earthly science being a still youthful reflection of that in the spiritual realms.

On Earth, science is confined to investigating physical matter and the forces that act upon it, without the obligation to explore the essence of the spirit, as each plane of reality examines its own matter and nature. However, when allied with philosophy, science allows the scientist and the perceptive scholar to be open to a broad observation of the whole, fostering the evolution of this system, regardless of beliefs or disbeliefs. After all, science is a system grounded in experimentation and hypotheses.

Neglecting hypotheses due to excessive scepticism turns the scientist into a perpetuator of stagnation. When science aligns with excessive profit or the acquisition of patents, it distorts the noble ideas transmitted to scientists through studies in spiritual planes while their bodies rest, as well as the intuitions they receive while awake.

May earthly scientists recognize that their knowledge originated from hypotheses and that their observations depend on technological instruments. Without hypotheses and instruments, they would wander without being able to proclaim that science is the light guiding humanity along the path of knowledge.

Above all, may humility allow them to unravel the still-hidden mysteries, without the presumption of having all the answers, for, on this planet, even the most advanced scientist is, in terms of knowledge, like a child in the cradle.

Selfishness

The difference between good and evil is revealed in the amount of selfishness present in our hearts. For those who attain greater awareness—those whose illusions of the world no longer hold sway—the clarity of the distinction between good and evil is more pronounced.

"Evil" arises from selfishness, manifesting when a being deliberately isolates itself in its own sphere, ignoring the ripple effects of its actions on others. Whether through harm, killing, or slander to secure personal comfort; whether by stealing, exploiting, or betraying for self-gain; or even if it does not inflict direct harm but contributes little or nothing to others, the focus remains solely on personal gratification. In such cases, it is selfish; it is evil.

"Good," on the other hand, shines in any action that places the well-being of others above one's own interests. It is the heart that, in any circumstance, seeks to avoid suffering, deprivation, or harm to others and the world.

The essence of every action that considers others is good, while evil is the shadow cast by the relentless pursuit of personal satisfaction, with no regard for the pain of others.

As a being frees itself from the shackles of selfishness, in both minor and major decisions, it draws closer to its angelic essence, reflecting the masters and disciples we so admire.

The most primitive of all behaviours, selfishness keeps us bound to animality. Hand in hand with greed-fuelled madness, it thrusts us into endless reincarnations, with the aim of eventually freeing us from this scourge.

All the evils of the world are rooted in selfishness, for all crimes and injustices are the offspring of selfish individuals who consider only their own opinions, desires, will, and pleasure.

Acting and thinking for the benefit of others is a sign of our elevation, drawing us nearer to divine grace.

May the selfishness still so present in us give way to generosity, and may we, in moments when we detect any trace of selfishness within us, do the opposite to finally eradicate the last drop of this poisonous evil.

Sex

Sex between two people is an energetic exchange that balances both sides, as each person possesses the pattern the other seeks. In couples who care for each other, sex occurs to deepen their connection. Over time, as they engage repeatedly, this bond strengthens, and the desire for additional encounters tends to diminish.

A lack of desire in a long-term relationship is not a sign of disinterest or lack of love, but rather an indication that both parties are already fully united in the flesh, making the continuation of sexual activity unnecessary.

Sex outside a stable relationship, though fleeting, still has the power to establish connections and energetic exchanges. However, as such relationships do not sustain an enduring emotional bond, the magnetism between the parties dissipates over time.

Modern mystics often ascribe an exaggerated spiritual significance to sex, teaching that it somehow connects individuals to their higher selves and can be a means to enhance spiritual or even psychic abilities. While sex does involve the energies of physical, etheric and astral creation, it should not be mistaken for a tool to transcend its intrinsic purpose. Sex, ultimately, is more grounded in earthly experience than in spiritual realms. Spirits that dwell slightly above the average earthly spirit do not engage in sexual activities typical of Earth; for them, sex it is an instrument used by younger spirits, not out of malice, but for procreation and pleasure.

Excessive guilt about sex can lead an individual to believe they are generating karma, when, in fact, they are merely repeating an emotional pattern from the past. Sex, even without a lasting relationship, is not wrong and does not generate karma. Karma is only generated when harm is done to another, whether physical, emotional, or moral.

Those who use sex to control or gain advantages attract similar consciousnesses that vampirise their sexual energies in search of experiencing what they can no longer feel without a physical body. Often, in the afterlife, those who have corrupted sex in that way tend to face challenging situations.

Sex is sacred, but not necessarily spiritual, and it should be practised only when there is genuine desire or the purpose of creating, whether children or energetic threads that reinforce the bond with a partner.

Sleep

Sleep is a sacred rite, where our earthly bodies rebuild and our soul prepares for the dawn. In the softness of the night, as we rest on a serene and clean bed, the atmosphere should be pure and tranquil, far from the disturbances of heavy meals, bright lights, and arguments that disrupt peace.

During sleep, the energy that resides within us loosens the bonds between the physical and astral bodies, allowing the spirit to detach from the earthly shell. In this state, our consciousness roams the spiritual realms, seeking what truly resonates with our inclinations. Aligning our thoughts with light before sleeping connects us to our spiritual guides, who lead us through lessons, tests, recreation, and counsel.

However, those who lie down with the worries of the material world still lingering in their minds find themselves drawn to spheres where these anxieties dominate. Most, like many others, remain anchored to the energetic field of their sleeping place, mentally trapped by tense earthly concerns. The result is a morning filled with deep exhaustion, as though the soul found no rest, despite the hours of sleep.

Cultivate the habit of visualizing your body bathed in a white light, as if you were a powerful lamp, before surrendering to rest. Energy follows thought; thus, the light you visualize has the power to cleanse and strengthen the spirit.

Communicate with your spiritual guide or entities that elevate the mind, such as Jesus, Buddha, Krishna, or any saint. Offer your prayers, express gratitude, and send out wishes of love for the world. This brief moment of relaxation while lying down prepares the way for peaceful sleep, guiding the spirit on a joyful journey through the night.

Sleep is as essential for the spirit as wakefulness is for carrying on with daily life.

Sorcery

Both the physical and non-physical, or invisible, worlds are made of energy. Some are composed of dense matter, others of subtle or radiant matter. The manipulation of the more subtle matter of each plane of existence, when forged for evil, is called sorcery.

Directing these energies for selfish and malicious purposes causes these same invisible molecules to cling to the spirit, and they will only detach when what has been done returns to the sorcerer, who purges the harmful molecules through the experience of pain.

Many believe they control spirits, thinking they are their servants or friends, when in fact they are deceived by these lying entities. In the afterlife, they end up enslaved by them, having been tricked into believing in a false friendship.

We are given the great gift of reincarnation, and beyond the life and body bestowed upon us, many other resources appear without needing to resort to low magic to obtain anything. Magic that aims to harm others will unfortunately cause more than one lifetime of setbacks for those who pursue such means, for whatever is thought, felt, or done against another first imprints itself on the spiritual bodies of those who send it.

If incarnated humans knew how powerful they are, they would not use sorcery to harm anyone, for the great power they have to do harm is revealed in the weight of that harm when it returns to them. With such power, we can envision peace, tranquillity, prosperity, health, joy, and even love.

Let us forget our primitive past, both the one that recalls the early days of the caves and the one that connects us with vile consciences that still linger in the deepest zones of the spiritual plane.

"A man reaps what he sows," taught the beloved Jesus, reminding us that we are responsible for everything we do, that divine justice plays no favourites, giving to us what we give and taking from us what we take.

Spirituality

The knowledge we acquire should be used to spread the truth. Accumulating vast knowledge is not a passport to a glorious afterlife, as if those who study become special or favoured by enlightened entities.

The knowledge we can absorb while on Earth is limited, as both our physical brains and our current level of spiritual progress do not allow us to comprehend complex information beyond what the astral or lower mental realms can offer.

Those who are deeply knowledgeable should recognize that individuals considered uneducated, illiterate, or unaware of spiritual realities might, in fact, be spiritually more advanced than they are. Moreover, many exceptionally intelligent spirits in spiritual matters choose to reincarnate into lives of simplicity and ignorance, opting to grow in areas they had previously overlooked.

Those who study spirituality and esotericism should also apply the teachings they learn. Above all, humility is the principle that should be sought by those who have access to a glimpse of the real world.

Yet, even the wisest knowledge may fall short of truth; the divine beings we honour are not bound to any single religion. Mastery of spiritual ideas does not grant us passage to a higher heaven or a place of exaltation among the enlightened. Spirituality, too, should never be wielded as a means to conquer or possess, but rather embraced with humility and grace.

Knowledge used solely to enhance the ego, without being gently disseminated, is like a seed kept in storage, waiting for its planting.

Spiritual Treatment

Spiritual healing is the assistance that comes both to those who seek it and to those who are ready for it.

In spiritual healing, we are either alleviated or completely cured of an ailment that was inevitably caused by ourselves. By asking for help, we are developing a part of ourselves related to faith, which then makes room for us to understand that we are responsible for what happens to us, including the beneficial things.

One who is healed after spiritual treatment was already in the process of healing before the treatment. Thus, spiritual healing appears in our lives, whether through someone's intervention or through what seems like mere chance or coincidence. Therefore, healing does not come only to a few fortunate souls who live near healing groups or spiritualists, while others, less fortunate, suffer for not knowing about these healing places or for living in countries where such therapies are little known. Those who live far away or who spend their lives without hearing about spiritual healing know, deep within their spirits, that spiritual healing through conscious seeking is not something they are meant to experience in this lifetime, for various reasons related to their own paths.

The spirit is the matrix of the physical body, and the mental body defines and maintains the astral body. Healing of the spirit, or the subtle mind, reflects healing in the denser bodies.

Spiritual healing can commonly occur through the true prayer of the individual. However, if healing happens, it is because, deep within the being, they have been mentally refining themselves in response to the imbalance that caused the illness.

The mind, in our current state in the flesh, is the root and seed of everything.

Doing good generates great merit, which we use to obtain the blessings of healing. Thus, healing does not depend solely on the kindness of the medium or sensitive person, or even on payment to the paranormal, but exclusively on the merits we accumulate to free ourselves from such trials in advance.

The current life is the most important existence we have and is the chance to heal wounds from other lives. Today is the opportunity for everything that comes our way.

Only those who wish to be helped receive assistance, and by asking for help, we open ourselves to the possibility that selfless friends may act, according to divine mercy. God, in His infinite love, works through spiritual friends with mercy in our healing.

By receiving mercy, we learn to be merciful.

Whoever knocks on God's door will always find it open, and healing, even if partial or delayed, is achieved whenever we ask for it.

One Hundred Messages From Above

Stealing

Theft is not confined to large sums or valuable items; it also includes the small pilferages made throughout a lifetime.

A person who routinely takes a little here and there accumulates, over their earthly journey, a significant and valuable amount of what they have stolen. This total, in its entirety, will be exacted by the law of return. If a market stall sets a price for a certain weight of grapes, but the buyer adds a few extra grapes to the bag, by the end of their life, they may have stolen the equivalent of a vineyard.

Karma accumulates and can be exacted gradually or all at once. Thus, someone who took just one or two grapes from the stall may end up losing valuable possessions through theft, accidents, or fraud.

Similarly, the exploitation of a worker who, unable to refuse work, accepts a lower payment than expected also brings a significant karmic weight. The selfish contractor of poorly paid work may experience semi-slavery until they learn that taking advantage of others is a form of theft.

Honesty must be practised both in small matters and in more significant situations, as the laws of the universe remind us that even the possessions of the rich are subject to the forces of divine nature.

If we have taken something from someone, we should return it. If we can no longer return it, we should make amends through charity to those in need.

But above all, if you are stolen from, lift your hands to the heavens in gratitude, for it is better to be the victim of theft than to commit it yourself.

Sublimation

As the incarnated spirit follows the path towards God, it distances itself more and more from animalistic instincts and lower feelings.

The sublimation of the soul, akin to a stone shaped by the river's currents on Earth, is achieved through conscious inner reform. Gradually, we replace heavy foods with light portions of vegetables, complaints with words of tenderness, cruel habits with healthy hobbies, and arrogance with genuine kindness. We can choose to eliminate from our lives everything we recognize as toxic or primitive.

An elevated spirit carries many others towards the supreme good, whether through mental influence or the merits acquired, which can be exchanged for blessings, cures, and rescues for our loved ones.

May cruel traditions be abandoned, making way for

a fraternal culture; may disregard for nature be replaced by care and appreciation for all forms of life; and may our criticisms be transformed into vows of improvement.

Let us strive to accelerate our spiritual ascent to avoid repeating the same mistakes and facing the same sufferings in future lives. Let us purify our spirits with every opportunity we have. Even if our progress is small, we will have lived a life of growth rather than remaining in spiritual stagnation, repeating the same errors of many past lives, and staying in spiritual infancy.

Little by little, let us change, for the ant that advances steadily is worth more than the hare that never leaps.

Subordinates

Favouritism based on material possessions or earthly titles, showing courtesy to some but impatience and rudeness to others, reveals that the spirit is not prepared for any sublime role after its time on Earth. There are no superior groups of incarnated people on Earth; everyone is so alike that, most of the time, divine assistance happens collectively, without special treatment for those with more wealth or prestigious professions.

In the afterlife, upon entering adaptation colonies, our service will not start as doctors, psychologists, judges, or teachers. We will take on roles like cleaning assistants, attendants, or other dignified yet marginal jobs, starting from the bottom. Through these experiences, we will gather knowledge, paving the way for more complex roles in the real world after the period of humble service.

Let us treat our subordinates with kindness, for in the spiritual realm, when we depart and begin our service on that plane, we will also be subordinates.

Humility not only demonstrates kindness and gentleness of character but also conscious intelligence, reminding us that, as humans, we are still small and lacking in morality. The janitor, the shop clerk, the waiter, the cook, the street sweeper, the housekeeper are never below anyone because of the work they do. Woe to those who feel superior to them, treating them with contempt, for remorse will come, followed by a plea for an equivalent position, before the offender believes they deserve the forgiveness of those who were humiliated.

None of our actions will escape divine justice, which records all events in our own conscience. If we treat some disrespectfully today, based on their professional or servant roles, in future lives we will long for humble, often humiliating service, so that we may learn, in practice, what those who suffered at our hands went through.

The world turns, and the rich and poor always alternate roles in the dramas of reincarnation. Let us, then, choose humility and sympathy, so that, in the turning of the wheel of life, we may encounter humble and sympathetic superiors, capable of seeing us with the same respect we once offered to those who were beneath us.

Suffering

Human suffering is the experience of pain, but also a purifier of debts.

Our suffering arises when there is still a lack of acceptance of the unfolding effects caused by the actions we set in motion. There is no punishment, only neutral laws that allow our spirits to learn through pain, which serves as a vehicle for awareness, meaning that pain makes the individual more conscious.

Suffering should not be a choice, but if it arises, may it be faced without the need for others to share the same pain.

Others are never responsible for our suffering, for divine justice, unlike human justice, is not blind. The one who endures suffering without allowing it to turn into guilt or pain for others can understand that their own pain, like their debts, is nearing an end.

Pain awakens the individual to the realization that

something needs to change. Without pain, many would continue indefinitely without improvement, without change, without evolution, driven by inertia or lesser desires.

For the enlightened spirit, all past suffering holds meaning, just as the adult engineer understands that the tears shed in kindergarten and nursery had their own reason for being.

If we cannot learn through the kindness we can offer, we will learn through pain. And once the pain subsides, we may reflect that what we called suffering was a warning to bring about change.

Karma often presents itself as aspects of suffering or pain so that adjustments can be made to our own spirit, shaping it much like a baby who, before finding balance on two legs, experiences countless falls.

God never abandons those who suffer. Even those who choose their own suffering, out of remorse for a dark past, find relief in lighter burdens and shorter periods of pain.

The afflicted may knock at God's door, for it will open.

May the suffering of others be an opportunity for us to relieve it selflessly, for the suffering we ease is the cup of water our own thirsty souls will drink in moments of drought.

Suicide

Those who commit suicide destroy the vehicle but not the conductor.

Released unnaturally from the body, suicides often relive the moment of death in a continuous cycle in the spiritual realm. Upon finding themselves trapped in the state caused by suicide, they continue to experience the same reasons and emotions they had in earthly life, though now only on the astral plane.

Unfortunately, in many cases, this agony persists until the time originally intended for that incarnation runs out. For example, if a person was meant to live approximately 55 years but takes their life at 30, they may endure the remaining 25 years in a death-like state. This happens because the vitality meant for a longer life needs to be expended. In certain situations, these individuals may reincarnate and pass away naturally at an age that corresponds to the remainder of the life expectancy from the previous incarnation, thus completing the interrupted journey.

When a loved one has committed suicide, prayers in a religious or spiritual temple are always the best remedy to ease their state. Praying at home may attract the suffering spirit to the location, affecting both them and those still incarnated. Depending on the merits of the one who passed and those praying for them, merciful spirits may rescue the sufferer more swiftly.

It is not uncommon for a suicide to have taken their own life in previous existences, being invited to face the same trials, yet failing again. It is also common for tormentor spirits to influence, through mental impressions, individuals with this history to commit suicide again. Therefore, if suicidal thoughts arise, we must transform them, ignoring negative images and choosing better ones.

Help should always be sought when thinking of suicide, both from specialists on Earth and from beloved spiritual friends. Let us remember that there is always a solution, and that the spirit never dies.

In moments of despair or loss of hope, invoke the Almighty—whether it be God, Jesus, or a spiritual master. Always remember to call upon them, for the response will come, and it is enough to want to live, even minimally, for an avalanche of help to arrive quickly.

Telepathy

Telepathy, the silent language of thought, permeates our encounters and dialogues, even without our awareness. Beyond the words we speak, the mental emanations we emit carry a deep responsibility, as we are constantly communicating telepathically with those around us.

In unconscious telepathy, our ideas, desires, and opinions reach other minds, shaping their feelings and decisions. However, when trying to forge or influence another's path with strong mental impressions, we may invade their free will, altering their intentions—an act that, at its extremes, manifests as spiritual obsession from one incarnate to another.

Care must be taken when interacting mentally with others, something that is always inevitable. If we interfere with others' thoughts, we open doors for other spirits to do the same to us while remaining blind to their presence.

Obsessive spirits, in the subtlety of their malicious actions, use telepathy to guide the steps of incarnates, who often do not perceive the invisible agent manipulating them. In many cases, we are their puppets without even realizing it.

In everyday interactions, it is natural to wish that someone acts according to our desires. However, if words fail, let a brief and sincere prayer flow from our hearts, asking for the best to manifest, both for ourselves and for others.

Ethics, that divine guiding star, instructs us to respect the sacred space of each being, always prioritizing the common good.

Lies may hide among words but not among minds.

When we lie, we know that, deep down, the truth has already been revealed to the other.

When we think ill of someone, we are communicating through toxins in the form of spears, throwing poisoned darts that wound not only the target but also ourselves. The negative signal we emit first corrodes our own spirit before reaching the outside.

If we happen to read others' thoughts without them wishing to communicate, let us keep that secret with wisdom and silence, never using it for personal gain or harm. The responsibility that comes from telepathic knowledge is greater than that obtained through physical means.

As we relate to human beings, animals, plants, and consciousnesses from other systems, let our mental conversations always be sources of pure and uplifting intentions, for we can mask the spoken word, but never the thought sent.

One Hundred Messages From Above

Temptation

Temptation occurs when we feel a strong urge to do something considered immoral or wrong, which we believe or feel we shouldn't. In most cases, these urges are produced by our own spirit, more precisely by our astral bodies, and in far fewer cases, by obsessive spirits.

The astral body is made of astral matter, which varies in density. When an individual is accustomed to engaging in something wicked, immoral, or regrettable, their astral body, where their coarser desires and emotions reside, remains in a denser form. Astral matter does this to maintain its cohesion within a body and, thus, have more power than it would if it were loose. In other words, astral matter seeks to densify as much as possible and, to achieve this, exerts pressure on the individual so that their lower, and therefore denser, desires manifest.

The more we indulge in worldly passions, excesses, toxic addictions, and diets of meats, the denser the matter of our astral bodies becomes. However, when we resist these pressures, this dense matter begins to dissolve, replaced by more subtle matter.

Conditioning to harmful habits is not only the result of the lower mental body but also the physical mind, generated by the physical brain. However, stronger than the mind or lower mental body is the astral body, which is the most influential subtle body for the incarnate individual.

Disembodied spirits, attracted by our vibrational similarities, can intensify this temptation, but it is essential to understand that we ourselves are the authors of these affinities.

Ultimately, we are responsible for all the impulses that emerge, as well as for being victims of lower spiritual. The temptation we believe comes from outside actually springs from within us. Therefore, inner reform is crucial, as it transforms the most hardened and shadowed parts of our being into light and lightness.

It is preferable to try and fail than not to try at all. Resisting temptation, even if we eventually succumb, is a positive step, as with each resistance, however small, the astral body is further sublimated.

Temptation is a test, and each time we resist, we earn points toward spiritual elevation.

Thoughts

The dynamo of existence is thought, which weaves the entire reality of being, from the essence of bodies to experiences in the various vibrational planes of existence. Thinking is not an incessant philosophical elaboration but the art of organizing mental matter, deciding which images should be avoided and which should be created or repeated.

When we shape reality through thought, it does not mean that we can alter all situations in our lives, including those that transcend the afterlife, as we are still subject to reality according to the degree of our evolution. The more enlightened we are by the altruistic character and compassion we exude, the more powerful our thought becomes in creation.

Thought travels any distance without weakening on the journey.

Thought is almost as enigmatic as God, and believing that we fully understand its essence is a materialistic illusion.

When we feel unwell, depressed, sad, frustrated, or enraged, it is important to avoid overthinking. Thought, when associated with negative emotions, can create an even darker reality, as we tend to give more importance to unhappy ideas than to those that promote hope, forgiveness, and contentment. Additionally, malevolent spirits, taking advantage of vibrational alignment, can approach and infiltrate our thoughts, amplifying their harmful forms or introducing even darker ones into our mental field. Therefore, it is advisable to distract ourselves with reading, music, contact with nature, interaction with animals, and prayers.

Thinking ill of others, wishing them harm, or deliberately constructing cruel images in our mind contaminates the mental body, which will inevitably have to purge these toxins through painful inner experiences.

"Watch and pray," said Jesus, warning of the temptation that affects the flesh through thought.

Thinking is being, and we are the reflection of what we think. But above all, thought is action, which, whatever its quality, will always find its reaction.

Timidity

Extreme shyness often reveals an individual who, in past lives, may have been blamed for something. Their timidity manifests as an unconscious feeling of being judged for past mistakes.

Many of us may have lived lives where we carried heavy secrets or were exposed for shameful acts at the time of death. The impression of guilt and embarrassment deeply marks the spirit, resulting in shyness as a way to prevent the individual from repeating their mistakes or to make them aware of their past transgressions, thus hindering their progress.

An extremely timid person is already in a state of remorse and is on a path of correcting their errors.

It is important to note that being reserved should not be confused with extreme shyness. However, every form of shyness reveals traces of previous lives, which may or may not manifest in the current life.

Leading an honest life and adhering to laws and the highest moral values can help the shy individual, as can meditation and exposing oneself to situations that might cause embarrassment. However, this condition, deeply rooted in the astral body and human DNA, is likely to persist, albeit weakened, until the moment of disincarnation.

Tragedy

Tragedies, which manifest as collective disasters, are the effect of what that same group caused, perhaps in times long forgotten.

Collective karmas occur for the renewal of souls, and never for the places where they happen. The souls involved in tragedies, whether due to human or natural causes, often choose the lesson that reveals their duty.

Those who seem to have the least resources often appear to suffer the most. However, it is the responsibility of those with many resources to rescue them, using divine grace and financial means to save lives. The poor, victims of the tragedy, are not victims but sufferers who drink from the cup filled by their past conduct.

Although accidents are common in physical worlds and do not relate to complex karmas, large tragedies involving many people at once are invariably the result of collective atonement. However, the spirits going through the tragedy in groups are not necessarily of the same evolutionary level; many may be merely purifying their last spiritual stains from a very distant past, while others might be participating in atonement to address a significant remaining debt to the universe's laws of balance.

Let us pray for divine mercy, which always relieves us, and practice good now to lessen or even avoid, through acquired merits, the possibilities of painful atonements.

Tragedies are not punishments but natural events aimed at eliminating the coarsest emotions of those who, in a sad past, caused similar suffering.

May the compassion of the survivors be greater than the cause of the tragedy, and may love inspire everyone to teach and learn to care for one another, for the greatest tragedy is not loving.

Traumas

Traumas are part of the learning process for the incarnated spirit, which experiences shocking and painful situations to relive, through striking memories, what it has caused itself.

All emotional processes are recorded in the astral body, where thought captures signals and stores them until they can be drained by this body. A trauma is, most often, a memory of past events triggered by a new, similar event. Trauma is the memory of emotion, not thought, with thought merely being the trigger; thus, the crystallized or old emotion seeks to be released.

Those who are traumatized are not necessarily deserving of the trauma but are its unconscious creators. In this way, the incarnated spirit relives, in the terror it possibly inflicted on others, the terror on its own skin.

The healing of trauma in the physical mind can be achieved through psychological and neurolinguistic therapies but first occurs in the spirit when trials are overcome. Trials and mental tortures eventually wear out, freeing the individual from the painful situation. On the other hand, those who suffer may choose, in spirit, to carry the trauma throughout their lives, taking the opportunity to learn through psychological pain, due to the remorse each person carries.

All emotional problems can be alleviated by helping others and by forgiveness. Helping others—whether strangers, those in need, animals, or nature—creates healing currents in the spiritual body, torn by trauma, that dissolve the forms of trauma and irregular mechanisms present in the mental field. The light that emanates from each cell when kindness is practised mechanically reduces the imbalance caused in the universe.

May the traumatised be blessed by God, and may they bless everyone with their help and affection, for the good we do today reduces the harm we caused yesterday.

Truth

Truth goes beyond simply being the opposite of spoken lies; it is the essence of living in authenticity and being who we truly are. Often, we navigate our lives guided by the opinions and judgments of others, spending an entire existence speaking, dressing, working, and seeking truths that others want to see and hear. Thus, the illusions of the spirit manifest not only in what we say but in our actions, habits, and personality.

Lies, when devoid of malice and without intent to harm, become a shield protecting us from the exposure that truth would bring, allowing us to escape others' judgments. However, speaking and acting in truth, despite possible consequences, requires the courage to face the contempt of those who prefer illusion over the simplicity of truth.

Truth is recognizing that we are not defined by our

current state; we are merely passing through. Lies, on the other hand, make us believe that our present form and condition are true and eternal.

Stay true to your spirit, rather than acting according to the expectations imposed by the world's hypocrisies. Truth is not merely revealing the opposite of lies but being faithful to who we truly are and wish to be. And before speaking the truth to others, let us first speak the truth to ourselves, remembering not to change or act according to the illusory world's expectations.

Vanity

Captive to the worship of physical beauty and the body, for millennia, we have delayed our progress toward true personal evolution. Attachment to material possessions inevitably reflects an attachment to our own physical appearance, which, though fleeting, is often considered one of the most important aspects of our existence.

We confuse healthy bodies with showcases, where energy and resources are abundantly spent to maintain a constantly radiant display, as if we were trophies proclaiming: "We are worthy because we are beautiful."

Desiring to be beautiful or to remain youthful is, in itself, a healthy pursuit and does not oppose spiritual evolution. However, when the worship of image becomes excessive and physical appearance takes centre stage in our lives, it is like going to school and only worrying about the uniform we wear, without concerning ourselves with studying or learning.

After disincarnation, those who lived a life deeply rooted in vanity often find themselves in dense spheres of existence, lost and disbelieving that their lives were merely superficial and without purpose, having dedicated so much attention to something that has been left behind on Earth. In other cases, not uncommon, the spirit struggles to detach from the physical body, which is no longer a functioning vehicle, and, due to mental and emotional magnetism, remains attached to the corpse, even during decomposition.

As physical beauty often becomes a great temptation for vanity, diverting the spirit from the path it promised to follow, these spirits, in subsequent reincarnations, request to acquire less attractive bodies according to prevailing beauty standards. They may also request glandular or DNA dysfunctions, choosing to reincarnate with some imperfection in appearance, so they may live a life that distances them from attachment to illusory beauty and avoids using appearance for manipulation.

May we be healthy and attentive to our appearance, seeking to be beautiful inside and out, but never forgetting that outer beauty is a reflection of inner beauty. The more we try to be beautiful while ignoring our moral flaws and our commitment to good, the more we risk attempting to compensate for the lack of inner beauty with exaggerated means to achieve external beauty.

Wakes

The suffering caused by the apparent loss has, over millennia, led us to develop wakes, where we try to say goodbye to our loved ones. In our grief, we cry around the coffin, light candles, and fill the air with melancholy over what has happened.

For the deceased, however, this situation can be one of great anguish and, above all, fear. Many who pass away do not know how to deal with the weight of these rituals and the sad energies directed at them. Not all spirits can quickly detach themselves from the energetic ties of the body and free themselves from the mental influence of those still in the flesh.

Mourning is an experience that must be lived, but holding a vigil over a body can be a form of torture for the spirit that wished to remain alive, even though, over time, they understand that there was no intention to increase its suffering. Excessively invoking the dead, whether out of longing or inability to accept their departure, can keep them bound to suffering. For this reason, spiritual guides may create distractions for the living to divert their attention to greater matters, thus freeing the newly deceased from the harmful energetic ties of those mourning their departure.

Donating the organs of the loved one can give others the chance to live longer and better. This is not only an act of compassion towards others but also a merit for the spirit itself, even if they did not make the decision to donate.

Cremation is an honourable act; however, it is important to wait at least 48 hours after death.

May God and the spiritual friends bless and assist everyone in this difficult moment and guide the deceased toward the vastness of the real life that awaits them.

And may wakes and funerals be replaced with sincere prayers of hope, so that sorrows may lessen and understanding may reach everyone's hearts.

War

Wars are the physical reflection of the mental creations on the planet. The hatreds generated by thoughts, words, and actions form a repugnant mental mass that seems to hover over the individual and, when it comes to groups and nations, over everyone in that place. Often, these thoughts are the result of collective karma, born from animosities generated in past existences.

Unfortunately, wars affect the peoples who, both in the present and the past, have fostered conflicts. And although our dear brothers deserve all help, they often experience war again, albeit on the opposite side, thus alternating their defences with each new existence.

Sufferings on Earth, including those where humans cruelly harm and exploit defenceless animals, intensify the forces that manifest wars in the physical world. Spirits of low stature, driven by desires for revenge, control, and rebellion, influence peoples and, especially, the leaders of countries, through almost enslaved workers.

Although the financial and technological conditions of some nations are well established, the primitivism of the spirit still manifests, as war arises when morality is low.

God does not abandon us and invariably alleviates conflicts, while His lofty workers of light mobilize vast resources to mitigate large-scale conflicts. However, the inhabitants of Earth, blinded by the desire for revenge and others' exploitation, unconsciously reinforce conflicts, resurrecting the past and shaping the future.

In wars, everyone is guilty, but everyone is also deserving of divine mercy, as no one will remain in ignorance forever.

May peoples dedicate themselves to weakening the forces that generate wars, forgiving those who can be forgiven and ceasing selfish exploitation.

In every thought, word, or action against others, we are feeding the lords of war.

Wars do not need to happen, despite the still significant karma of peoples. It is necessary that at least one-third of the population involved in a conflict decides, through forgiveness, that peace is the best for all, thus renouncing the illusory gains that war provides.

Wealth

Money is a tool meant to circulate and create in the physical realm. While acquiring large sums and desiring prosperity are not contrary to the divine, it is essential to understand that if wealth crosses our path, it should serve to help others, not merely as a celestial gift for a comfortable life.

Wealth carries with it a responsibility; no one is born on this planet solely to enjoy a life of abundance and luxury.

Unfortunately, many of the extremely rich have forgotten that the fortunes they inherited or acquired were planned in spiritual realms before their birth, with the purpose of promoting positive changes in the lives of those who have nothing, contributing to the improvement of the world, and regenerating the one who performs charity.

No one comes to Earth to experience being the life

of the rich, but to manage large sums for the benefit of a world that has long suffered from inequality.

Large sums of money are sacred not because they are a gift or a blessing, but because they are a tool entrusted to some by divine law. Fortune is meant to assist them in their spiritual progress, enabling them to help others through charity and detachment.

A great responsibility rests on the rich, as many do not use their money for the true purposes for which it was given. Owning a home, eating well, and having money does not spiritually harm. However, accumulating wealth or acquiring numerous luxury items in a world where many are starving is discordant with the purpose of incarnating, especially if that wealth is not used to alleviate one's own past misuse of resources.

May our prosperity also flow to others, for we will receive in double what we give. This does not mean we will receive double the money we give away, but rather double the kindness we choose to practice.

The greatest reason humans reincarnate so many times on Earth is precisely selfishness. Therefore, let us be happy to use our wealth to ease the suffering of those who still live in misery. Both the poor and the rich can enter the kingdom of heaven, in the more subtle astral planes, but for the rich, it is more difficult, as the commitment is greater.

Let us be rich in love, prosperous in fraternity, and live the luxury of making the lives of others happier.

Words

Words serve as constructive tools but, unfortunately, can also become destructive instruments. Harm arises not only from aggressive words but also from unpleasant expressions and curses, all linked to groups of unhappy beings in various planes of reality.

Profanities, mocking scorn, and verbal retaliation wound the speaker's spiritual body, leaving scars scattered throughout. The sound vibrations generated persist in the astral body, even after the physical waves cease. When we speak negatively about someone or expose others' flaws in their presence, we repel any positive energies that might otherwise be coming our way.

Even when not spoken with negative emotion, such as using a harsh word to express exaggeration or intensity, these words still carry an unpleasant weight in more subtle planes.

Words have the power to build with praise, humble teachings, and gentleness. On the other hand, rude comments and expressions of anger, words conveying atrocious emotions, carry thorns and pins, detectable by a skilled clairvoyant. Undoubtedly, these sharp points first affect the speaker and, to a lesser extent, the listener.

In the face of insults, we should cultivate kindness and reject the feeling of offence. Those who insult and offend are out of control, expressing their pain verbally. Understanding others' lack of control helps us avoid suffering without seeking revenge.

Both the offender and the offended are still in the early stages of their spiritual journey.

Let us nurture the sweetness, calm, and beauty of words, recognizing that they are the initial physical manifestation of thought, and that thought shapes the worlds we inhabit.

Work

Work and service are distinct concepts. Work refers to employment or duties that sustain a profession, a business, or livelihood, while service involves providing assistance through one's own efforts. Ensuring the well-being of ourselves and our families is sacred to our existence. However, the world often seems consumed solely by work aimed at maintaining status, acquiring luxurious possessions, and preserving appearances.

In our complete dedication to professional work, our physical bodies and living conditions, entrusted to divine law for our spiritual evolution, become tools that feed the mechanisms of material gain, leaving us with little time or energy for serving the world in a fraternal way.

We come to seek jobs and professions that, rather than nourishing the soul, only serve to enhance our comfort and status.

It is true that work purifies, and a salary is a blessing, but both need to go hand in hand with uplifting service. Let us not spend our entire lives merely working to accumulate possessions or gain recognition from others.

May our work also be a path of relief and dedication to others.

If in our business we offer a discount to the less fortunate, we are not just renouncing profit; we are receiving a burst of invisible lights emanated by the grateful heart. If we extend our hours to assist a late customer, we are not just exceeding the mandatory journey; we are cultivating the patience we will one day expect from others when we are the ones who are late. And when we employ someone, let us not try, at all costs, to gain advantages or the lowest price, for the exchange will always be fair, and we will receive what we give.

A life of service is not just dedicated effort for others; it is a life with purpose. What we take beyond this existence are the lessons learned, the tests overcome, and the memories built.

The countless hours spent solely on personal comfort and image will vanish like shadows at sunrise.

While on this physical Earth, let us work for what cannot be touched, for regret in the beyond is more real than any material treasure.